I0820158

love lessons

a modern guide to showing, giving, and receiving love

love lessons

a modern guide to showing, giving, and receiving love

ALISE MORALES

illustrated by

ANA JARÉN

ABRAMS, NEW YORK

CONTENTS

INTRODUCTION:

RETHINKING THE ORIGINAL FIVE LOVE LANGUAGES

Zodiac signs. Attachment types. Enneagrams. Love Languages. These days there are so many different ways we try to package and explain the unique blend of preferences, past experiences, motivations, and fears that make up our personalities. I'm a millennial woman, who came of age in the *Buzzfeed* era, so I'm no stranger to the siren song of a personality quiz. Yet, as I've grown and matured, I've often wondered if these rigid ways of understanding ourselves are actually helpful, or if they could be creating barriers where bridges could be built instead.

For example, I love astrology as a way to learn about myself, connect with a higher power, and understand more about people who think or act differently to me. Because I've written two books on the subject, I often get asked to perform at astrology-themed events or to give my thoughts on astrology-related topics. (Side note: please don't ask me to guess your sign at a party. I'm a Taurus and hate being wrong.) Usually, it's all in good fun, but every once in a while I'll run into someone who uses astrology as a way to write off other people or assume knowledge they can't possibly have. For instance, social media is littered with memes about how you should "never date a Scorpio," or how "a Virgo man" will inevitably do you wrong. Sure, some of these may be tongue-in-cheek, but they speak to a larger problem with our society's current obsession with personality categorization. As much as these identifiers can be used to celebrate individuality, they can also be used to classify, box in, or dismiss anyone whose "type" you've decided

10:00 pm

is not compatible with yours. Suddenly, something that was meant to help us understand and relate to each other better has become a wall standing in the way of deeper connection.

So, why am I talking about astrology in the introduction to a book about love languages? Because I've started noticing the same pattern happening here. *The Five Love Languages*, first published by Dr. Gary Chapman in 1992, gained popularity as a framework to help couples better understand each other. Since then, the five love languages that Chapman introduced (words of affirmation, quality time, physical touch, receiving gifts, and acts of service) have become ubiquitous in dating culture. While many still use them as a tool to create deeper understanding between their partner and themself, for others they've become yet another way to put a stop on a relationship before it has even started. *His love language is words of affirmation, but mine is acts of service? It can never work! She likes receiving gifts, but I'm not a gift-giver. Time to pack it up!* To be clear, this was not the original intention of the love languages, but in a time where dating apps allow us to screen for every possible personality difference before we even say hello, I fear they've become yet another way for us to write off a person before we've even met them. Once again, something created to help us better understand and celebrate our differences has suddenly become a tool for quick judgment and easy assumptions.

When I talk about "rethinking" the love languages, in many ways I mean going back to their original purpose as a tool for understanding and empathy. In the world of the love languages, no one language is considered superior to another. They are all equally valid ways to express love, meaning no one is a better or worse person for preferring one over the other. Starting

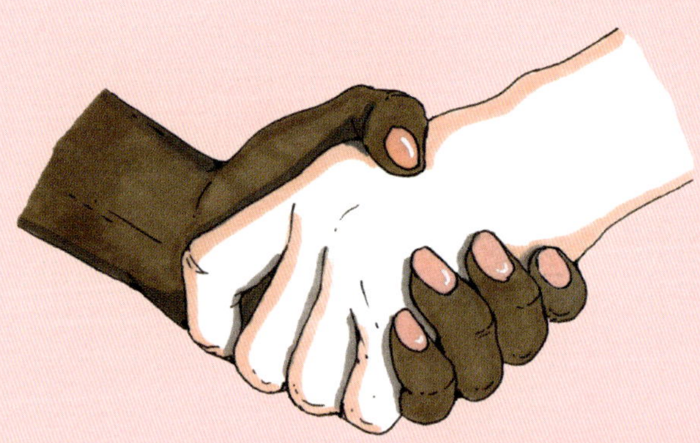

from this place of equality, we can all approach learning about someone else's preferred love language from a place of open-hearted understanding, knowing that their expression is just as real and relatable as our own. In this book, we're also going to try to stop seeing our love language as a singular, set-in-stone identifier for how we like to give or receive love, and instead see it for exactly what it is: a preference. The idea that every person has *only* one way that they like to experience love is simply untrue, and thinking that way could make us fail to recognize all the wonderful expressions of love we see around us every day—not just from our romantic partners, but also from family members, friends, coworkers, and even random people we pass on the street!

WE'RE GOING TO STOP SEEING OUR LOVE LANGUAGE AS A SINGULAR, SET-IN-STONE IDENTIFIER FOR HOW WE LIKE TO GIVE OR RECEIVE LOVE.

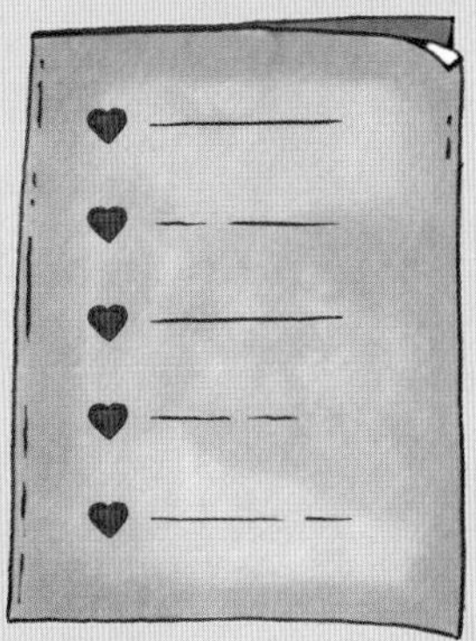

So, we're not only rethinking the love languages, we're also expanding them. First, we'll talk about how our understanding of the original five love languages can be updated for modern relationships. Then, we'll add a few more love languages to our "menu of love" so that we can work on even more ways to express love to those closest to us. Finally, we'll take a look at how the love languages apply not only to our romantic relationships but also to all the other people in our lives. At the risk of sounding clichéd, love truly is all around us. We just have to keep our hearts open enough to see it.

PART ONE:

LOVE LESSONS FOR THE MODERN ERA

Want to feel old? 1992 was thirty-three years ago. In this section, we'll be taking the original five love languages and updating them for the internet age, taking into account queer couples, non-traditional relationships, and neurodivergence. We'll also be adding a few new love languages of our own—because who doesn't want more ways to love?

THE FIVE LOVE LANGUAGES TODAY

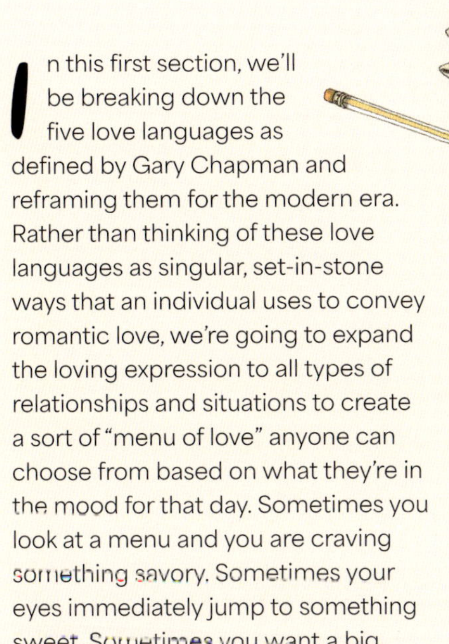

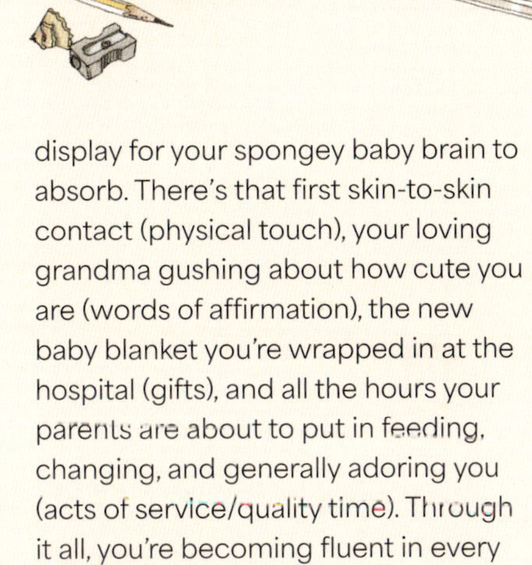

In this first section, we'll be breaking down the five love languages as defined by Gary Chapman and reframing them for the modern era. Rather than thinking of these love languages as singular, set-in-stone ways that an individual uses to convey romantic love, we're going to expand the loving expression to all types of relationships and situations to create a sort of "menu of love" anyone can choose from based on what they're in the mood for that day. Sometimes you look at a menu and you are craving something savory. Sometimes your eyes immediately jump to something sweet. Sometimes you want a big, rich plate of pasta, while at other times you want to sample a variety of light appetizers. (OK, now this metaphor is making me hungry . . .)

Humans are fluent in all of the love languages. From the moment you're born, all of the love languages are on display for your spongey baby brain to absorb. There's that first skin-to-skin contact (physical touch), your loving grandma gushing about how cute you are (words of affirmation), the new baby blanket you're wrapped in at the hospital (gifts), and all the hours your parents are about to put in feeding, changing, and generally adoring you (acts of service/quality time). Through it all, you're becoming fluent in every love language from your very first day on earth.

Of course, we all have preferences, but the theory behind this book is simple: love languages should be seen as options, not rules, and as with any other language, it's good to be

IT STANDS TO REASON THAT THERE WILL NEVER BE ANY SINGULAR WAY THAT WE WANT TO RECEIVE LOVE.

proficient in more than just one. As Dr. Chapman says, "The number of ways to express love within a love language is limited only by one's imagination." I agree! And that's why I think it's high time to reframe the love languages, not only for the modern era, but for all the varied relationships where love and respect can serve as a foundation.

Chapman's love languages were originally conceived for romantic relationships, so that's where we're going to start. For many people, finding romantic love and building a successful romantic relationship are core to living a happy life. There's a reason why *Bridgerton* is one of Netflix's most-watched series, or why people still love the 2005 adaptation of *Pride and Prejudice*, most ardently. We humans love love! We love to give it, we love to receive it, and we love to watch it play out between beautiful people in Regency-era attire.

But how do we keep romantic love once we get it? This has proven to be one of life's trickiest questions. Many of us have had to learn the hard way that simply liking someone a lot or being attracted to them does not a working relationship make. These days, confidence in dating has reached an all-time low, thanks to a phenomenon called "dating-app burnout." One Forbes Health survey found that 80 percent of millennials (born 1981-96) reported feeling burnt out by dating apps "sometimes, often, or always." Those numbers weren't any better for other generations: 79 percent of Gen Z (born 1997-2012) reported feeling the same, alongside 78 percent of Gen X (born 1965-80) and 80 percent of baby boomers (born 1946-64).

Those who experience this burnout reported feeling exhausted by the constant stream of new faces and lack of connection. This data may seem bleak, but underneath the burnout I see something promising: people *want* to build successful relationships. Sure, there will always be the serial daters who "aren't looking for anything serious," but the majority of people in the dating pool—regardless of age, gender, or orientation—are there because they want to meet someone special and build a connection.

That's what the love languages are all about—building connection by creating a shared language of love. There are infinite ways for us to connect with each other, and what

builds connection one day may not be what is needed the next. We are all complex, dynamic people living complex, dynamic lives. It stands to reason that there will never be any singular way that we want to receive love, because there's no singular way in which we show love to others.

Which brings us back to our "menu of love" metaphor (you might want to get used to it). The chances are, the deeper you get into a relationship, the more you'll learn about your partner's preferred love languages. You may even be able to guess most days what they'll be ordering off the menu. You'll learn that after a long day your partner wants nothing more than for you to help with the dishes, or that their favorite way to spend a Sunday is cuddled up on the couch. In turn, they'll learn about the types of compliments you find most meaningful, or the look you get on your face when you really need a hug.

However, there are always days when, for whatever reason, we want something new on the menu. Perhaps it's been so long since you had salmon that you've forgotten what it tastes like, or a sudden health kick has you ordering the salad. The point is, for over thirty years, we've had the same five options on the love-language menu. They're great options! We love ordering them, but now it's time to add some new entrées to the list.

So let's put on our chef's hats and get cookin'! (Gordon Ramsay would be so proud.)

REFRAMING WORDS OF AFFIRMATION

Let's start our reframing exercise exactly where Dr. Chapman starts in his book: words of affirmation, or, words used to express love, appreciation, and respect for another person. And let me just say, reader, that you are looking absolutely *dashing* today. And look how many pages you've read already! Genius alert!

It's hard to argue against words of affirmation. Who doesn't like being told they're great? There's even science to back it up! Some MRI evidence suggests certain neural pathways are increased when people practice self-affirmation tasks, while studies have shown compliments light up the same part of your brain as when you receive a monetary reward. (Though monetary rewards are always appreciated [insert my Venmo here].)

The Five Love Languages describes words of affirmation as "powerful communicators of love" that come with multiple "dialects." The three dialects are:

- Encouraging words.
- Kind words.
- Humbled words.

Once again, it's hard to argue against being encouraging, kind, and humble in all your relationships, but it's important to remember that words of affirmation should also be genuine, backed by action, and never come at the expense of another very important person: yourself.

WORDS OF AFFIRMATION TODAY

One of the first lessons we learn as a child is to be kind to others. Kind words and encouragement can go a long way in helping us all to be better people. But in today's society, we also have more of an awareness of who is disproportionately expected to always put kindness first, even when anger or frustration is warranted: women.

Women in heterosexual relationships are often expected to be their partners' constant cheerleader and companion. At work, they're expected to sugarcoat their language to avoid hurting the frail egos of coworkers. As any woman or person who has spent any time living as a woman will tell you–it's exhausting!

We can all agree that leading with kindness and empathy is a great virtue, while also acknowledging that expectations around who is allowed to–as us '90s kids would say–stop being polite and start getting real, changes based on a person's gender or gender expression. People from marginalized groups are always going to have less leeway to express anger, give a harsh critique, or even simply be straightforward about their needs and expectations. Black women, in particular, are subject to this kind of tone policing.

WORDS THAT MATTER

There is always going to be value in building someone up—particularly a romantic partner—and helping ensure confidence. As someone who struggles a lot with self-criticism, I can't count how many times words of affirmation from my partner, friends, or coworkers have helped build up my own confidence.

However, it's also important for partners to be able to express hurt, anger, and frustration without feeling as if they've betrayed the other person or failed in the partnership. (Once again, it can often be women who feel this pressure in their relationships.) People are allowed to stand up for themselves, and they're allowed to be angry when they do it. Sure, there are always going to be times in a relationship when partners try being the bigger person and letting the small stuff slide, but what about when a partner has done real harm? It's OK for partners to make demands of each other, be honest about each other's faults, and state clearly how those faults affect the relationship.

Partners shouldn't let the desire to shower each other in words of affirmation prevent them from being honest or asking for what they really need. Just a few examples of reasonable demands partners can make of each other are:

- "You have to stop drinking."
- "You need to get a job."
- "You need to start investing in our shared future."
- "You need to improve your communication with me."
- "Your hygiene habits need work."

How many relationships have failed because one person felt as if they couldn't actually communicate what they want from their partner? How many have languished in unhappiness, waiting for unmade demands to be met? Certain demands, when lovingly made, can do more to strengthen a relationship than a lifetime of service to the idea of being low maintenance or accommodating (another burden that can often be disproportionately placed on women with male partners).

WORDS THAT WORK

Sometimes words aren't enough. Everyone loves to hear kind words of encouragement, but if they're never followed by actions, they can sometimes ring hollow. Even if you have a partner who strongly identifies as a "words of affirmation" person, words alone will not always be a salve for every issue they put forward. Listen closely to what your partner is saying, and if what you're hearing is stress or overwhelm, the best way to show love may be with an act of service to take something off their plate—or even a gift that will simply make them smile.

There are also times when the person doing the affirming is simply doing too much. They're laying it on thick, and frankly, it's making the other person a little uncomfortable. It's one thing to be complimented, it's another to be fawned over. Sure, we all love to have someone sing our praises, but hearing the same tune over and over again can make it lose its luster. You may feel elated the first time your new partner brags about you to their family, but if they do it over and over again at every subsequent meeting, you might actually start to feel embarrassed.

> EVERYONE LOVES TO HEAR KIND WORDS OF ENCOURAGEMENT, BUT IF THEY'RE NEVER FOLLOWED BY ACTIONS, THEY CAN SOMETIMES RING HOLLOW.

You may have heard the term "love bombing" come up in online conversations around relationships and dating. The term refers to a form of emotional manipulation in which one person showers another with excessive attention and affection to gain their trust. This is an example of when words of affirmation are weaponized into a tactic of abuse, and is something people who are actively dating should be on the lookout for, particularly in the early stages of a relationship. Anyone using words of affirmation as a way to suggest they're the sole person on the planet who would ever view you in such a positive light is not actually expressing love, they're establishing control. It's not just a red flag—it's a blinking red light with an accompanying airhorn screaming at you to get the hell out of there as quickly as possible.

In short, there's a time and a place for everything. While words of affirmation are nice, sometimes quiet action is preferred, or even a direct confrontation is warranted. Like everything else we discuss in this book, time, place, and context are key when deciding whether to build someone up or give them a reality check, which can actually end up being more of a kindness than sugarcoating things will ever be.

REFRAMING QUALITY TIME

Quality time is another love language that is universally understood as being part of the foundation of any successful relationship. In *The Five Love Languages*, it's defined as "giving someone your undivided attention," and is assigned three dialects:

- **Focused attention.**
- **Quality conversation.**
- **Quality activities.**

Every relationship should include some element of quality time. Without shared activities and experiences, it's almost impossible to build a truly fulfilling life with another person. Even negative shared experiences like the "romantic" ski trip that ended with a broken ankle, or both of you ending up with food poisoning from the all-inclusive buffet, can strengthen a connection—or at least become a beloved inside joke.

Exactly what quality time looks like will differ from partnership to partnership. How you spend quality time with one significant other may not be how you spend quality time with your next partner. What quality time looks like between two people (or a group of people) will depend on the individuals involved, and can be anything from a quiet night in watching movies to a three-day hike along the Appalachian trail. The only rule when it comes to quality time is to make sure it's meaningful to everyone involved.

REFRAMING FOCUSED ATTENTION & QUALITY CONVERSATION

When *The Five Love Languages* defines focused attention and quality conversation, the book makes it very clear what that looks like. According to its original definition, focused attention means conversations in which both people are making eye contact, and listening intently without engaging in anything else. For the majority of people, that's exactly what focused attention and quality conversation will look like! But there's a group of people for whom those things might look a little bit different, especially in the context of a loving partnership in which both people need to feel comfortable letting their guard down and being themselves. I'm talking about neurodivergence.

Fun fact: I have ADHD. This manifests in my life in a variety of ways (some fun, some not so much), but one of the big ones is that it makes me a fidgeter. When I was in school, I'd always doodle in the margins of my notebook while my teachers were talking—drawing little concentric circles or filling in tidy squares. Many of my teachers took this as a sign that I wasn't paying attention and scolded me for it. What they didn't realize was that keeping my hands moving in this way

was the only way I could pay attention. The moment I was stopped from being able to draw my little circles, my brain would go haywire trying to burn off the excess energy that had previously been used by moving my hands. Suddenly, my ability to pay attention was nil.

The moral of this story is simple: I should have gotten a better grade in math. Just kidding (but if my ninth-grade algebra teacher is reading this . . . there's still time to make it right).

The point is, attention looks different for different people, and that is tripled when it comes to the belief still held by many that attention means eye contact. For people on the autism spectrum, making and maintaining eye contact can feel like torture. When they're forced to do so, much like when I was forced to stop my doodling, all their brain's energy is focused on that, and not on what the other person is saying.

The concept of "masking" for neurodivergent people means the time-consuming, and often exhausting, process of hiding your neurodivergence for the sake of others' comfort. While this may be a necessary skill at the workplace, or in certain social settings, neurodivergent people shouldn't have to mask for their partners, or when they're in the comfort of their own home. In a truly loving relationship, the partner of a neurodivergent person would adjust their understanding of "focus" and "quality conversation" to include their partner's unique expression of it. Listening looks different for different people, and allowing for this divergence will actually lead to more fulfilling quality time for both parties.

> **THERE'S NO ONE WAY TO SPEND QUALITY TIME.**

LEARNING TO LOVE QUIET MODE

In my own marriage, my husband and I alternate between who is in what we've lovingly dubbed "quiet mode" based on how we're feeling on any given day. In general, I identify as a talkative person. (Just ask all my teachers, who reliably noted "talks too much in class" on all of my early-grade report cards.) I'm a comedian, so it really should come as no surprise that my default setting is to chat about anything that comes to mind. But when I'm feeling overwhelmed, I immediately flip the quiet-mode switch and could happily spend an entire day not uttering a single word. The same goes for my husband (who is also a comedian—go figure). The key to navigating this is open communication. When one of us is in quiet mode, we'll give the other a heads-up, usually in the form of a text that says, "Quiet mode today. Feeling a little off. Love you." Acknowledging the capacity for these modes in both of us, understanding that there are days when certain types of quality time are off the table, and learning to accept when our modes are not aligned wasn't easy, but the result has absolutely strengthened our marriage.

So what do you do when both members of a partnership are in quiet mode? That brings us to . . .

Reframing Quality Activities

What type of millennial would I be if I didn't push back a little bit on the idea that screens automatically mean low-quality time? When both partners are in quiet mode, sometimes the best type of quality time they can offer each other is to wind down while watching their favorite show.

I mean . . . think about it! How many couples do you know who have "their show" that they watch together religiously? Just ask them what would happen if one member of the partnership watched the latest episode without the other if you doubt the importance of this type of passive bonding activity. And it's not just couples! The prevalence of watch parties for all sorts of things, from sports games to *RuPaul's Drag Race*, to the *Succession* finale, shows just how much communal watching of a screen can create a sense of togetherness. The point isn't what you're doing, it's how you're doing it. As long as both people are engaged, there's no reason an evening in front of the TV can't be a meaningful "quality" activity. At the end of the day, it's all about giving time–a.k.a. a little bit of your life–to someone else.

The point is, there's no one way to spend quality time, and no version of quality time is inherently more valuable than another. Sure, hiking a mountain together is impressive, but bonds can also be formed over dinner, on a long car ride, or even just chatting over the phone for an hour or so. The type of quality time you enjoy is always going to be different for different people. Ideally, you'll find a partner who has roughly the same definition as you, but the chances are that expectations around what counts as quality time will have to be adjusted to meet each other's needs. The only thing that quality time *has* to be is enjoyable and fulfilling for all parties involved. Even just twenty minutes of sitting beside each other in silence, enjoying a show you've committed to see through together, can be a gift when one partner (or both!) is feeling a little overwhelmed.

And now that we've said the "G" word, it's time to talk about . . .

REFRAMING RECEIVING GIFTS

Receiving gifts can sometimes get a bad rap as the selfish love language, but this couldn't be further from the truth. A thoughtful gift, given at the right time, has the ability to totally brighten a partner's day and is a great way to show that they're on your mind even when they're out of sight. Gifts are used across cultures as a sign of respect, and most marriage traditions include some kind of gift exchange.

Gifts don't have to be expensive, or even cost anything at all. The point isn't to show off your own wealth or thoughtfulness. The point is to give a person you care about a small token to let them know they are loved and appreciated. Some ideas for thoughtful, inexpensive (or free!) gifts include:

- **A pretty rock or flower you picked up on your way home (so long as it's not from someone else's property!)**
- **A cute card from the drugstore with a handwritten note.**
- **A coffee from their favorite place, made just how they like it.**
- **Pizza picked up on your way home from work.**

GIFTS THAT MATTER

Let's be honest . . . we've all received a dud gift before. From too-small clothes, gifted by an aunt who refuses to believe you've grown up, to obviously re-gifted bath soaps, or moldy leggings from your cousin's latest multi-level marketing scheme, gifts have just as much power to show thoughtlessness as they do to show someone you care. I always remember the childhood Christmas when my dad gifted my mom a telescope—something she'd never once indicated she wanted—then proceeded to use the telescope himself for all of the time we owned it. Clearly, he wanted an expensive telescope and had used Christmas as a way to justify the purchase. Obviously, this was not a gift that made my mom feel seen, and we still poke fun at him for it to this day. (To be fair to my dad, he's usually a great gift-giver. The siren song of an expensive telescope to a man in his mid-forties was simply too great to resist!)

There are also those who try to use gifts as a way to avoid tough conversations or well-earned apologies. We all know the image of the husband who has done wrong coming home, hat in hand, to deliver flowers to his wife. In this scenario, he hardly has to say a word before the wife scoops up the flowers and throws her arms around him, whatever it was that made her mad now magically forgotten. But sometimes the best gift you can give someone you've wronged is a genuine, heartfelt apology. Flowers to say, "I'm sorry," are great, but they should come with an actual "I'm sorry," as well. Without it, the flowers can quickly

start to feel like a shallow bribe–as if one partner has assessed the other's pain to be worth roughly $10, plus the cost of gas. It doesn't feel good, and it defeats the purpose of a gift.

Of course, gifts can be a beautiful way to bring joy to your partner's life and show them that you care. When someone says that they love gift-giving, oftentimes what they mean is that they love the way giving a gift makes them feel. These people aren't giving gifts out of a sense of obligation, they're doing it out of a genuine desire to bring happiness to someone that they love. There's a reason people will often refer to gifts as "a token of my affection." That's precisely what a gift is supposed to be! It's something that you give to someone else as a symbol of your affection for them. The best gifts aren't the ones that are the most expensive, they're the ones that display the most affection. Gift-givers will often tell you there's no greater high than the look on someone's face when they open your gift and realize you remembered the scarf they pointed out last time you were out shopping, or that you remembered the name of their favorite artist and got them a print.

On a recent episode of the podcast *Normal Gossip,* former host Kelsey McKinney told the story of a daughter who was sure that her father's Christmas gift of a custom ham bag for mom (yes, you read that right, a bag for carrying ham) was going to be a disaster. Instead, her mother burst into tears on Christmas morning, absolutely thrilled by her husband's gift. As it turns out, his wife had wanted a new ham bag for their Christmas ham (this story takes place in Australia, by the way) and had specifically pointed out this very bag as something she really wanted. Was the ham bag expensive? No. Was it particularly glamorous? I guess that depends on how much you associate glamour with ham. But the gift remains one of the mother's prized possessions, lovingly cleaned by hand after each use–not only because of its ability to properly store and protect a ham, but because it showed that her husband had been listening and internalizing even her most innocuous comments.

People who identify with the receiving gifts love language shouldn't let this get in the way of seeing all the other ways that love is expressed. The extravagance or frequency of gifts in a relationship is not necessarily related to how much someone loves you or cares for you. Remember that gifts in the love language sense mean small tokens to show that a person cares. Becoming obsessed with the size or frequency of gifts means that you may miss all the other little things that your partner does to communicate their love—from taking out the trash when it's supposed to be your day (acts of service), to posting a positive comment about you on Instagram (words of affirmation), to the little squeeze they give your arm when they walk by, just to say, "hey" (physical touch). Gifts are one way to express love between partners, but they're not the only way.

GIFT-GIVING & SELF-LOVE

One way to reframe the love language of receiving gifts is to simply remind yourself that a gift doesn't always have to be received from someone else. You can give yourself gifts as an act of self-love. Whether it be a little treat picked up on your way home from work or a bouquet of flowers to brighten up your workspace, picking up something for yourself is a great expression of self-love. As I'm writing this, in the fall of 2024, there is a trend going around on TikTok called "she deserved the purse." The trend started after an image began being shared far and wide of a small, inexpensive purse left on a shelf in the babycare aisle. The image told a story that rang true for many women—of a mother who sacrificed buying a small item for herself in order to make sure her baby had what it needed. The image, emblazoned with the words, "she deserved the purse," eventually racked up 25 million views on TikTok and prompted a wave of spontaneous, selfless gift-giving, as women began hiding small amounts of cash or notes of encouragement among the baby formula and diapers at department stores, in the hopes of encouraging the parents (mainly assumed to be moms) who might find them.

"She deserves the purse" is a powerful example of the value of gift-giving, and that original poster was right: she did deserve the purse, and so do you. (Or whatever purse-equivalent indulgence you've been denying yourself in service of everyone else.)

Speaking of service . . .

REFRAMING ACTS OF SERVICE

The Five Love Languages defines acts of service as "doing things you know your spouse would like you to do." With that definition out of the way it's time to come clean. I am an acts of service girl. Nothing makes me feel more loved and seen than when my partner takes something off my plate. As someone who chronically overbooks myself and ends up burning the candle at both ends, sometimes the only thing I want to hear when I'm on my way home is, "I'll handle dinner tonight," or "Don't worry about taking the dog on a walk." (OK, so my husband is the one who takes our dog on 90 percent of his walks, but my point still stands.) Not only do I tend to spread myself too thin, but I also have a very hard time admitting when I need help. If this sounds like you—welcome to the club! We meet on Thursdays.

All that is to say, acts of service make me feel profoundly seen. When my husband, a friend, or a family member offers to take on a task that I didn't even realize I was dreading, it shows me that they love me enough to be more in tune with my emotions than I am. Of course, I'm still a big girl who is responsible for using her words, asking for help when needed, and maintaining a manageable schedule, but the fact that I know there are people in my life who will step in and lend a helping hand when I am not able to do so, makes me feel not only blessed, but also safe.

That said, the fact that acts of service are my preferred love language doesn't mean I want acts of service all the time. We all know the feeling of wanting to vent about something in your life, only to have the person on the receiving end of the venting session go into problem-solving mode. All you wanted was for them to listen and let you blow off steam, but instead they've sprung into action, making suggestions and offering solutions that you've already considered yourself.

Just as with every other love language, the idea of doing something for someone else has a time and a place. Sometimes the most effective act of service is to simply sit and listen (i.e., sometimes the best act of service is actually quality time). That's why it's so hard to try and pin down your partner's primary love language. Once you dig deep, they all tend to bleed into one another: quality time can be an act of service, an act of service can be a gift, while a moment of physical intimacy can say, "I love you," as loudly and clearly as if the words of affirmation were spoken out loud.

ACTS OF SERVICE VS. CHORES

Where does the natural division of labor between partners end and acts of service begin? This was a question I grappled with often while thinking about this love language. Some things *The Five Love Languages* list as potential acts of service include:

- Cooking a meal.
- Setting a table.
- Emptying the dishwasher.
- Changing the baby's diaper.
- Walking the dog.
- Trimming the shrubs.
- Dealing with your landlord or insurance companies.

When I read this list, my answer is a big old "it depends." In general, an equitable household will split chores and tasks evenly based on each partner's abilities and inclinations. This may change slightly if one person stays home while the other works, but I'd argue that regardless of who identifies as the breadwinner, jobs such as changing the diaper of the human being you created should fall to both parents. That's not something you do for your partner. It's something you do because otherwise you'd have a baby that's covered in poop.

In my household, my husband tends to take on tasks such as doing the dishes, vacuuming, and walking our dog. I do most of the cooking, grocery shopping, bill paying, and deep cleaning of our bathroom. We both take on the laundry, kitchen cleaning, and tidying of spaces like the living room, bedroom, and home office. These are not acts of service. They're chores. And while we should always appreciate the things our partners do to keep our shared space comfortable and clean, they benefit both partners equally.

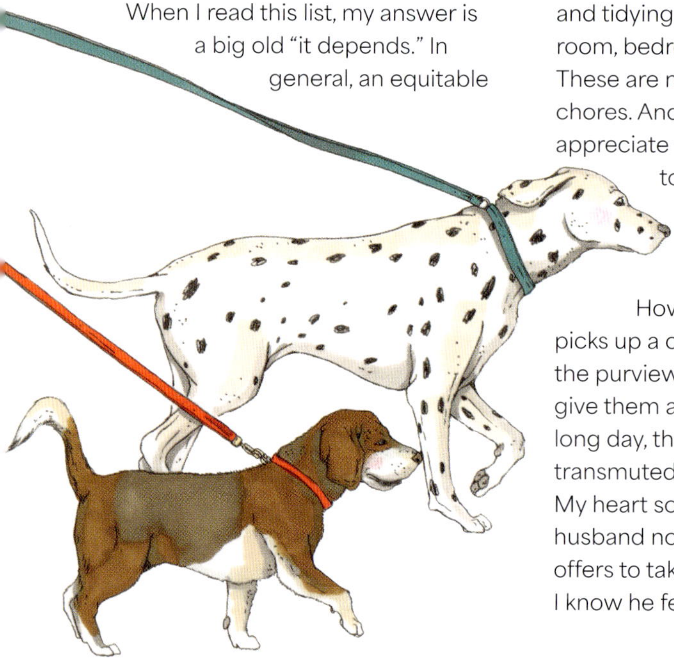

However, when one partner picks up a chore that is typically under the purview of the other in order to give them a break after a particularly long day, that chore is magically transmuted into an act of service. My heart soars on nights when my husband notices I'm overwhelmed and offers to take over making dinner, and I know he feels the same way when I step in and take over one of our dog's walks so he can relax. The difference between a chore and an act of service will be different from couple to couple. For heterosexual couples, it is important that they remember to keep gender dynamics and expectations in mind. Oftentimes, societal expectations around the role of wife and mother affect what is seen as their duty vs. what is perceived as going above and beyond. It's common to see a mom on social media lament the "you're such a good dad" comments that her husband gets when taking their kids to the park, whereas her own park attendance is barely noticed.

Again, you change the baby's diaper because the baby needs its diaper changed, not as a favor to someone else. (Except maybe yourself, as you'll no longer have to be around a stinky, crying baby.)

SELF-CARE & ACTS OF SERVICE

Just as we discussed in the section on receiving gifts (see page 24), acts of service don't have to be something you wait around for someone else to do for you. You can perform acts of service for yourself. Self-care may seem like little more than an internet buzzword these days, but it can also be a powerful way to show yourself love. If you find yourself constantly putting your own needs aside for your partner, your coworkers, your boss, or even your friends, it may be time to take a step back and offer yourself some acts of

service. Light that fancy candle. Turn off your phone and turn on your favorite comfort show. Draw yourself a warm, scented bath.

It is important that we take time to show ourselves love. As a partner, you should allow your other half the time and space they need to engage in acts of self-care that they find particularly nourishing. As RuPaul says, "If you can't love yourself, how in the hell are you gonna love somebody else?" When we take time for self-care and allow our partners to do the same, we're ensuring that everyone in the relationship feels nourished and whole. We all know someone in our lives who spends so much time doing for others that they barely have a second for themselves.

Everyone deserves to feel love, not just from others but from within. Love languages don't just flow from one person to another. They're things that we all have the ability to give to ourselves. With that in mind, it's time to move on to the final of the original five love languages, which also happens to be the one most in need of reframing.

REFRAMING PHYSICAL TOUCH

Now we get to the diciest love language of all: physical touch. On the one hand, physical touch is an important part of any intimate relationship. From the moment we're born, skin-to-skin contact is one of the first ways that humans learn to show each other that we care. Physical touch is such an important marker of intimacy between humans that all cultures around the globe have some form of it embedded into their ways of showing love and respect, even platonically—from handshakes to hugs, to kisses on the cheek. On the other hand, unwanted physical touch has the power to be annoying at best, and traumatizing at worst. To make matters even more complicated, the desire for physical touch is fluid and can change based on mood, time of day, place, or any number of other constantly changing factors. For example, we all know the kind of physical touch that a person is comfortable with in the bedroom is not necessarily the kind that they'd be comfortable with on a crowded bus or train—even if the person doing the touching is the same.

Physical touch, above all others, is the love language that is most likely to change based on a person's mood. Even someone who strongly identifies as being "touchy-feely" may find themselves suddenly not wanting touch that they'd previously welcomed. Massive life changes, traumatic experiences, or changing health conditions can all change the way we want to be touched, even by the people we love most.

In short, touch is a powerful tool for showing love to another person and is a vital part of any romantic relationship. The type of touch a partner enjoys will be very personal, and is shaped by many factors such as sexual preferences, past trauma, neurodivergence, cultural background,

among a whole host of others. So what does "good touch" look like? Good touch between intimate partners is welcomed by both parties and comes from a desire to give pleasure or comfort to another person.

Physical touch has been linked to health benefits such as stress reduction, lower blood pressure, and better immune-system function. One study in the National Library of Medicine even found that hugs may boost heart health. On an emotional level, physical touch can help to establish intimacy, trust, better communication, and improvements in mood through the release of oxytocin—sometimes referred to as "the love hormone" or "the cuddle hormone." Yep, that's right. Humans have a hormone that makes them want to cuddle. Oxytocin does lots of wonderful things for us and our romantic relationships. Our bodies release oxytocin when we're being sexually intimate with a partner *and* when we're cuddling in bed afterward. After giving birth, oxytocin floods the birthing parent's system to help facilitate bonding. It even helps move milk from the breast's ducts to the nipple to begin the breastfeeding process—one of the ultimate expressions of love through physical touch. However, just because oxytocin is helping the way, it doesn't mean a breastfeeding parent suddenly wants to be touched all the time. In fact, many mothers or birthing parents report feeling the opposite.

BEING TOUCHED OUT

One of the clearest examples of how the desire for physical touch can change over time is a phenomenon experienced by new moms/birthing parents called being "touched out." Giving birth to a child is (to put it mildly) an enormously complex physical experience. Even the "easiest" of births leaves new moms or birthing parents feeling exhausted, hormonal, and confused over their loss of bodily autonomy.

On top of all that, instead of being able to recover, new parents have to . . . well, parent. If they're breastfeeding, this can further the feelings of loss of autonomy, as their body is quite literally not just for themselves anymore. Between pumping, feeding, cuddling, and holding their new baby, it's no wonder some new parents report a feeling of sensory overload that results in not wanting to be touched at all by anyone, including their partner.

When we think of love languages as primary, unchanging parts of a person's personality, we fail to recognize that the way we want or need to be shown love can change over time. Does being touched out mean that someone who just gave birth doesn't love their new child or partner? Of course not! It just means that the way they want to be shown love has changed based on their circumstances.

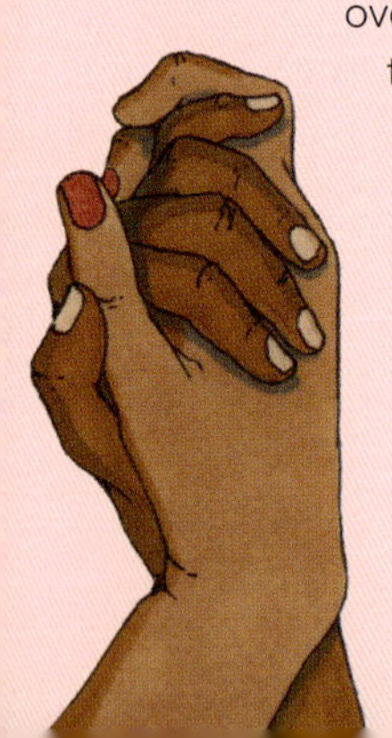

It can be jarring for a previously physically affectionate partner to pull back on that affection after a major life event such as birthing a child, but when we have a more fluid understanding of love languages as a menu of options for showing someone love, it's easier for partners to adjust. It also makes it easier for the person experiencing that touched-out feeling to move past the guilt and shame that often comes with it. If someone has spent their whole life saying their love language is physical touch, the sudden desire for physical space may lead to a loss of identity. But if they've always understood that love languages are subject to change, they'll see the sudden need for bodily autonomy less as a loss of self, and more as a reasonable change based on their circumstances.

PHYSICAL TOUCH & NEURODIVERGENT OR ASEXUAL PEOPLE

There are factors in a person's life that may make them relate to physical touch in a way that is dramatically different to others. For example, people with ADHD or autism can often experience hypersensitivity to certain types of touch, making it unpleasant for them or incredibly stressful. The point of using physical touch as a love language is to establish intimacy and comfort, so there's no reason to try to impose it upon a person for whom that is not going to be the reaction. Instead, try engaging your neurodivergent partner about the types of touch that do work for them, and try to build a level of physical intimacy that works for you both.

Equally, there are many misconceptions about how someone who is asexual feels in regards to touch. Asexuality does not necessarily mean that all levels of romantic touch are off the table, or that a person does not want to be touched at all. As with partners who are neurodivergent, if your partner is asexual, it will be important to decide together what your touch preferences mean for your relationship, and how you're going to be physical (or not) in a way that leaves everyone feeling safe and protected.

CONSENT & COMMUNICATION

Even a partner who usually loves physical touch may find themselves touched out. In this case, it may be better for their partner to show love with an act of service (taking over dinner prep or some other chore), words of affirmation (commending them on their adjustment to parenthood), or a gift (picking up their favorite postpartum snack on the way home). This adjustment actually displays love and care on multiple levels because you're showing your partner that you're in tune to their current emotions and boundaries, and willing to adjust to fit their needs.

Building a life with another person means being able to roll with all the changes and phases that life can bring. As with all things, consent and clear communication are key. Partners should feel comfortable telling each other when they're not in the mood for intimacy. On the flip side, partners on the other side of the physical-touch equation should be able to talk about how the sudden change in intimacy has affected them, and work with their touched-out partner to find a solution that leaves all parties happy and fulfilled. (Or, as happy and fulfilled as two new parents can be.)

Easier said than done, sure, but by reframing the love languages as options rather than rules, we can all learn to respect each other's desires and boundaries—even when they change.

NEW LOVE LANGUAGES TO EXPLORE

Alright, so now that we've explored and reframed the original five love languages, it's time to ask ourselves the same question that I always ask myself when choosing toppings at an ice-cream parlor—why limit ourselves to just five? Love is a complex, big emotion that we humans express and receive in a multitude of different ways, across a variety of relationships. While the original five love languages are great foundations that we can all use to communicate love in a romantic partnership, the reality is that the ways in which we humans give and receive love are as expansive as the emotion itself.

To bring it back to our "menu of love" metaphor, just like any restaurant is always adding new dishes to the list, I think thirty years of *The Five Love Languages* is more than enough time to add a few more options to our love menu. Of course, the old standards will still be available any time you want to order them (is there anything sadder than when a restaurant takes your old fave *off* the menu? It's just the worst . . .) but it's time to add some new recipes, flavors, and cuisines. When we let our love menu evolve, grow, and change, it means that we are also letting our relationships evolve, grow, and change with it.

Perhaps you've found that there is a relationship in your life where you feel stuck. No matter what you try, it seems that nothing is working or moving the needle forward. Sure, you could throw in the towel on that relationship, say you've tried everything, and move forward with one less person in your life to worry about, but we all know that's easier said than done. It may be easy enough to let someone go when the person we're talking about is an ornery coworker, less-than-friendly barista, or casual acquaintance who has shown that they're not someone you want to move up to true friend status. But what about when the relationship is really meaningful, such as a friend you've known for years, a romantic partner you live with, or even a member of your own family? When we're talking about the relationships that really matter in life, we all want to make sure that we've exhausted every option for repair before we call it quits.

So, why not give ourselves some more options?

Remaining static in our understanding of love is one way to ensure that our relationships get stuck in a rut—a.k.a. the death knell of all formerly successful partnerships. Everyone changes throughout their lifetime, so it stands to reason that when two or more people get together to create a partnership, that partnership will change over the course of their lifetime, too. If we keep reaching for the same five tools in the same old toolbox, we may find that all of them have lost their luster. Gifts, quality time, physical touch, words of affirmation, and acts of service may have worked just fine for years, but as we grow and mature, it may be time to add some new languages to our repertoire and see how they can help expand our understanding of partnership and expressions of love.

In this section of the book, I'll be introducing you to four brand spanking new love languages that you can use as tools to help strengthen your relationships. These new love languages reflect a more modern understanding of how we give and receive love in partnerships today, based on what we've all come to know about psychology, connectivity, social dynamics, and respect.

So, without further ado, the four new love languages I'm introducing are (drumroll, please) . . .

- Respecting Boundaries.
- Emotional Security.
- Healthy Debate.
- Shared Goals and Experiences.

As we work through each of these love languages, I'd strongly encourage you to pay attention to how they make you feel. If you find yourself having a fiercely negative reaction to a particular language, it may be because you've felt a lack of that language in your own life, or in a relationship

> **THERE'S NO REASON THAT THESE NEW LOVE LANGUAGES CAN'T BECOME YOUR GO-TO DISH ON THE MENU IN NO TIME.**

that is particularly meaningful to you. Chances are just reading these new love languages already has your mind spinning on how they can be implemented in your relationships. These words may even bring up big emotions for you as you consider how things such as disrespected boundaries or a lack of emotional security may have impacted you in your own life.

The truth is many of these new love languages have only begun to be established as markers of love and respect in recent generations. Understandings of love have changed dramatically throughout human history—from the courtly love of Shakespeare's time to the "father knows best" relationships of our grandparents era, and the dating-app courtships of today—and they'll continue to change throughout our lifetimes and beyond! The way our children build and think about partnership will likely be a little different (or even drastically different) to how we do, and suddenly it will be time for the love languages to be revamped once again! I'll be the old fuddy-duddy whose mindset needs a tweak (don't worry, I can take it. I'll be at a nursing home enjoying my third helping of pudding).

And guess what? These new love languages *still* don't represent all the ways we can express love and respect to one another. Perhaps as you're reading this, you'll realize that there's another new love language that's not expressed in this book or in Dr. Chapman's book that you want to explore. So, do it! Get in the kitchen and start testing out some recipes. Love and respect are big, complicated topics that are bound to bring up big, complicated feelings. The good news is that just because a relationship has lacked in certain areas in the past, it doesn't mean you cannot forge a new path for that relationship going forward. Realizing that a relationship is broken is the first step to repair and, as long as every member of the partnership is open, there's no reason that these new love languages can't become your go-to dish on the menu in no time.

RESPECTING BOUNDARIES

Ah, boundaries. Is this yet another buzzword doomed to be misinterpreted by TikTok therapists to mean some version of "I never have to do anything I don't want to do or that makes me uncomfortable in any way for any reason, ever?" Or is it something more? As you can probably guess, this book comes down heavily on the "something more" side of things. Which is why we've labeled "Respecting Boundaries" as our first new love language for the modern age! When we talk about respecting boundaries as a love language, what this means is being in tune with your partners' needs and personal history. It means truly caring about how your partner exists in the world and wanting to build a space for them in the relationship that feels comfortable and safe. It means understanding that they're a different person from you, and that they move through the world with different priorities, experiences, and emotional triggers.

A partner's boundaries will drastically affect how they engage with the original five love languages, even the ones they identify with most. If your partner is afraid of dogs, for example, surprising them with a new puppy is probably not going to go over well, no matter how many times they tell you that gifting is their love language.

Quality time is another love language that can dramatically change depending on a partner's boundaries. While hanging out on the couch and watching a three-hour-long war epic might sound like the perfect evening to one person, for a partner who hates loud noises, violence, or death scenes, it could be something akin to torture. (OK, so "torture" might be a bit hyperbolic, but you get what I mean.) That's why it's important to check in with your partner to ensure that what you mean by quality time and what they mean by quality time are at least roughly in sync. The point

is for the time spent together to be enjoyable for both people, and making sure you're aware of each other's boundaries is one useful way to make that happen.

When you think of the word boundary, it may conjure up the image of something that separates people from one another. However, in this instance, healthy boundaries are actually a way to bring someone closer. When someone shares a boundary with you, they are telling you something vital and deeply personal about themselves. They are sharing a vulnerability with you, in the hope that you will use the information to love them better. For example, if your partner tells you that they need space after an argument, it can feel like a rejection, but if you dig a little deeper into the request, you can find a meaning that is rooted in deep care for you as a person. What they're really trying to say is, "I love and respect you so much that I want to take time to sort out my feelings before we talk about this again so that I don't say something hurtful that I don't mean."

That's what setting and maintining healthy boundaries is all about—communicating love and respect.

Unfortunately, this can be easier said than done. Identifying what is a healthy, reasonable boundary and what is an unfair ask between partners can be difficult. Many of us have suffered from a lack of strong boundaries in our romantic, family, or work lives, meaning it can be hard for us to recognize and impose healthy boundaries in our romantic relationships as well. On a much darker note, there are also people who use the concept of "boundaries" as a way to control, manipulate, or confuse their partner into behaving in exactly the way that makes them feel best, regardless of how the request makes their partner feel. This misuse of boundaries is not a show of love or respect and is, in fact, a major red flag that should be paid close attention to in a relationship. It may be a sign that a breakup is in order.

HEALTHY BOUNDARIES VS. UNFAIR ASKS

I keep using the phrase "healthy boundaries," so naturally you're probably asking . . . what is it that makes a boundary healthy?

Healthy boundaries are limits that individuals put on their relationships to help them feel safe, valued, and respected. They're there to protect a person's sense of self as well as their physical and mental wellbeing. Healthy boundaries are things that we put in place for *ourselves*, not requirements that we place on other people. Healthy boundaries are set with "I" statements and are not rooted in an attempt to control another person's behaviors or way of life. You place boundaries for yourself. You don't impose them on other people.

For example, a partner who is working on improving their spending habits might say something like, "I'm not going out to eat this month." That's a healthy boundary that they are well within their rights to set for themselves, and a good partner would help support them in that effort by not tempting them with

invitations out to their favorite restaurants, or sulking when their partner holds firm and doesn't join them on a night out with friends. Where this boundary could get dicey would be if the money-saving partner also insisted, "And I don't want you to go out to eat at all this month either." Suddenly, this boundary has changed from a very reasonable self-focused "I" statement to a control-focused "you" statement that is bound to become a source of friction as resentment builds within the partner who isn't currently working toward the same financial goal. Of course, in a situation where finances are shared, all partners have to work together to come up with spending habits that they're comfortable with.

Some other examples of healthy boundaries that can be established in a relationship include:

- "I don't want to watch more than two episodes of a TV show in one sitting." This one has been established by my own partner—much to my binge-watch-loving chagrin.
- "I don't want to be around drinking/smoking/drugs."
- "I won't respond to texts after 10 p.m. on weeknights."
- "I will remove myself from any arguments that involve personal attacks."
- "I don't feel like having sex with you tonight."

On the flip side, examples of inappropriate or controlling false boundaries could be:

- "I need you to have sex with me once a day."
- "You have to be home by 10 p.m."
- "You have to answer my texts within fifteen minutes."
- "You can't be friends with members of a certain gender."
- "You can't be friends with your ex partner."
- "You can't wear outfits that I deem too sexy."

As you can see, healthy boundaries are "I" statements designed to help the person imposing them live a happier, healthier life. False boundaries are "you" statements designed to control another person to create maximum comfort for the person imposing them, with little regard for what it does to the person on the receiving end.

Now that we've got those definitions out of the way, it's time to talk about all the ways that respecting healthy boundaries set by your partner in good faith can strengthen a relationship and show love.

BOUNDARIES IN THE MODERN ERA

The idea of having strong boundaries has become more mainstream, opening up a major divide between older generations (sorry, boomers) and their more boundary-conscious kids and grandkids. For many in the baby boomer generation (born 1946–64), the idea of children having strong boundaries with family members was nearly unthinkable. Father knew best, you should always listen to your mother, and a good wife would never put her own needs (a.k.a. boundaries) ahead of those of her husband.

Thankfully, nowadays, all of that has changed.

Now, we recognize that a person's children have the same rights to put up boundaries with their parents (and grandparents, and nosy great-aunts) as they do with anyone else in their lives. Even millennials (born 1981–96) who grew up with boundaryless familial relationships are learning in therapy how to establish boundaries going forward, even against staunch pushback from family members who benefitted from the lack of boundaries before.

Scientific studies have born this out as well. A survey from 2022 of a thousand Americans conducted by the Thriving Center for Psychology, found that 58 percent of respondents reported that they have trouble saying "no" to others. That same study found—rather unsurprisingly—that women are far less comfortable than men with saying "no," with 63 percent of women respondents saying they consider themselves "people pleasers" vs. 58 percent of men.

> **Everyone is capable of learning how to impose and respect healthy boundaries.**

When it comes to generational breakdowns, things get a little bit more interesting. Gen Z (born 1997–2012) is generally known as the boundary-setting generation, and they have built a reputation for themselves as far more likely than any other generation to set boundaries at work or school. However, that same Thriving Center for Psychology study found that Gen Z was actually the *most likely* generation to attend events they didn't want to go to, followed by millennials, Gen X (born 1965–80), and baby boomers.

Clearly, the issue of boundary setting is complicated and can't be neatly broken down by generational divides. While Gen Z may be totally comfortable telling their boss something is inappropriate, they're less comfortable telling a friend they can't make an event, even if they don't want to go (FOMO can be a powerful motivator). Meanwhile, boomers are famous for their boundaryless work-life balances and struggle to receive boundaries set by younger family members. However, they have no problem staying home from an event they don't want to attend and are far less concerned with the social consequences. (One of the many freedoms of getting older, I assume.)

No matter what age group you're in, previous generations' ideas about boundaries (or lack thereof) can come into play when trying to create new rules for your romantic relationships. If you or your partner come from a family with extremely porous or weak boundaries, learning how to enforce your own boundaries and respect those of your partner can be a very difficult task. But don't despair! Everyone is capable of learning how to impose and respect healthy boundaries. As with all things, it takes open communication, vulnerability, and a lack of defensiveness to get it done. The first step is to simply put yourself in your partner's shoes and try to understand where they are coming from. Oftentimes, boundaries are deeply personal reflections of an individual's history, dating back to their earliest memories from childhood. For example, a partner who has strong rules around raised voices may have been traumatized at a young age by a parent or caregiver who yelled often. Even if raised voices don't bring up the same feelings of anxiety for you (some of us may come from families where "loud" and "louder" are the only volume settings), adjusting how you express yourself to accommodate your partner's feelings will communicate to them that you are a safe person to share their history with and that you can be trusted to take that history into account in your interactions with them.

Ultimately, that's what the respecting boundaries love language is all about—showing your partner that you see them and love them for who they are, and that their comfort is as much of a priority for you as your own.

HONORING BOUNDARIES (EVEN WHEN IT'S HARD)

Let's get this out of the way right up top: sometimes respecting someone's boundaries, even if you understand them or want to do what's being asked out of respect for your partner, can be tough. Boundaries are, by definition, an intensely personal thing. This means that something that may be a vital boundary for one person, can seem totally unnecessary or even ridiculous to another. For example, the partner who has a specific boundary against watching TV shows or movies with lots of gore or violence may be totally baffling to their horror-movie-loving partner. But when that partner agrees to keep their movie nights blood-free without constantly pressing the issue, they're showing their partner that they respect and love them for who they are—even if that means they host their scary-movie nights somewhere else. And if a love of scary movies is so important to one partner that they can't respect the other's boundary? That may be a sign that there is a fundamental lack of compatibility, and could mean that it's time to reevaluate the relationship and part ways in a loving, respectful way.

Another thing to keep in mind when it comes to respecting boundaries is that they are not necessarily etched in stone. Like all the love languages that we've discussed so far, boundaries can shift based on a variety of different circumstances. For instance, at the start of a romantic relationship you may have totally different boundaries around communication or physical intimacy than you do in the midst of

> SOMETHING THAT MAY BE A VITAL BOUNDARY FOR ONE PERSON CAN SEEM TOTALLY UNNECESSARY OR EVEN RIDICULOUS TO ANOTHER.

a years-long committed partnership. Blowing up someone's phone with texts at all hours of the night or holding hands in public may be big no-no's for someone at the start of a relationship, but totally normal behavior down the line. A key aspect of respecting someone's boundaries is also having enough grace to allow them to shift. This, of course, requires clear communication from both parties as to how and why a boundary has shifted, and if or when it may come back.

Once again, let's look at the example of a partner who has just given birth. We've already discussed how their relationship to physical touch might be completely upended by the birth of a child (see page 34), but that's just one aspect of their life that has changed. New parents may find that they have totally different needs around communication or rest, and have developed an entirely new tolerance (or lack thereof) for loud noises and clutter. When one partner tells another, "I'm going to respect your need for alone time right now," they are showing that partner that their needs are important, and in turn are making them feel more loved than they would if their partner tried to impose quality time in that moment, even if their partner had previously identified quality time as their most-beloved love language.

I have a lot of personal experience with this. Some of the most common boundaries that my husband and I set with each other are around time and space. As we discussed in the previous chapter, we often switch between who is in "quiet mode" in our relationship (see page 22). However, we're both responsible for communicating this with each other, so that everyone can get what they need without leaving the other partner confused or with emotional whiplash. Those conversations can look as simple as something like this:

ME: *"Hey babe—will be home in ten minutes. It's been a long day so I think I might just hang out in the bedroom and keep to myself for a bit to recharge. Thank you for understanding."*

HUBBY: *"No prob—let me know if you want me to throw some wings in the air fryer for you."*

It really is that simple! However, if you're really feeling anxious about boundaries in a relationship, one of the easiest ways to clear up any confusion is to just ask! Revolutionary, I know, but some people often forget that checking in is the simplest way to make sure you and your partner are on the same page about what is going on. Oftentimes, when we don't do this it's out of fear—a fear of rejection, fear of uncomfortable conversations, or fear that the simple act of asking might somehow hurt or upset your partner.

Here are some more examples of how conversations to establish and respect each other's boundaries could go:

PARTNER A: *"Hey, I'm really touched-out from watching the kids all day. Do you think you could give me some physical space?"*

PARTNER B: *"No problem. The left side of the couch is all yours."*

PARTNER A: *"I get really overwhelmed having serious conversations first thing in the morning. Could we hold off on this convo until after breakfast?"*

PARTNER B: *"Alright. Let me know when you're ready to chat."*

(NOTE: This last example doesn't mean Partner A has carte blanche to be a "Don't talk to me until I've had my coffee" person. Nobody has the right to impose total silence on someone else. What we're talking about here is being considerate of when someone is in the best mindset to engage in certain types of conversation, not demanding nobody say "good morning" until you're ready.)

> CHECKING IN IS THE SIMPLEST WAY TO MAKE SURE YOU AND YOUR PARTNER ARE ON THE SAME PAGE ABOUT WHAT IS GOING ON.

These examples are obviously best-case scenarios for how boundaries are communicated and received. Sometimes, the person establishing the boundary is so frazzled that the ask comes out wrong or overly aggressive, especially when they don't have much experience at creating boundaries in a respectful way. Sometimes, the person on the receiving end of the boundary becomes defensive due to their own inexperience with these types of conversations. In fact, fear over how a partner is going to receive a boundary is one of the most common reasons that someone might be afraid to establish one. It's natural to worry about how a conversation is going to be received, and the more you know or care about someone, the more weight will be given to fears around hurt feelings, and how your thoughts or emotions will be received. As someone who can hardly send food back at a restaurant without falling over myself with apologies, you can imagine how difficult I find having some of these conversations when the person on the other end isn't a server that I met ten minutes ago.

So, how do we get to a place where everyone in the relationship feels comfortable establishing boundaries, renegotiating them, or simply expressing how they feel? We'll talk about that with our next new love language . . .

Emotional Security

Everyone wants to feel safe expressing their emotions in a relationship. In fact, there's simply no way to build a healthy relationship with anyone—whether they be a family member, friend, coworker, or romantic partner—in which one person is being held hostage by the other's anger, anxiety, or emotionality. It doesn't matter how many gifts they give, the quality time you spend together, or that they can whip up the world's best chicken-noodle soup at the first hint of a cold—if you don't feel comfortable telling your partner how you feel, and they don't feel comfortable doing the same with you, there's just no way for either person to feel satisfied, safe, or secure. And what kind of partnership is that?

We all know the tyranny of life with an emotionally volatile person, whether it be the boss from hell, an ex you're never going back to, or a toxic friendship that you have had to leave behind. Firstly, these relationships are just plain exhausting. No matter what the good times look like, tip-toeing around another person's reactions because you're never sure how they'll handle criticism or bad news is a breeding ground for resentment. When a relationship is lopsided in this way, one person's emotional security may be given all the value, while the other's is left completely unattended.

Once again, I have to ask . . . what kind of partnership is that?

In a true, healthy partnership, both people feel comfortable talking about their feelings with one another, even if it means a tough conversation. As an avid reader of advice columns, I see this theme pop up over and over again from desperate partners begging popular columnists like Dear Prudence at *Slate* or Lori Gottlieb at the *Atlantic* for advice. The story always goes the same way:

Partner A loves Partner B, but they've grown so emotionally exhausted by Partner B's mood swings, anxiety, depression, or anger that they're no longer interested in a romantic relationship. They want to leave, but they know that as soon as they try then Partner B will fall apart, oftentimes going so far as to make threats of self-harm or even suicide if the relationship were to end.

This is the sad and frightening end that many people in relationships with a lack of emotional security find themselves in, and it causes heartbreak for everyone involved. As painful as it is, people are allowed to end relationships that they no longer want, and a relationship that both partners know they can safely end is, somewhat ironically, the only type of relationship that it is safe to continue. When we talk about emotional security, we mean a relationship with a foundation of strength, respect, and clear-headedness that allows everyone in the partnership to say what they think–even if what they think is that it is time for the relationship to end.

Emotional Security & Attachment Styles

If any time your partner expresses anger, fear, or anxiety, they are met with anger, fear, and anxiety in return, you are not providing them with emotional security. Think of this as the concept of giving your partner a "safe place to land." They can tell you what is bothering them—even if it's you—and know that they'll be listened to and met with a respectful conversation. That doesn't mean you have to agree with everything your partner says, but being able to have a civil conversation about tough emotions goes a long way toward showing you care.

Why do difficult conversations sometimes go so desperately awry? Some of it can be boiled down to yet another personality defining metric: attachment styles.

While attachment styles may seem like yet another pseudo-psychological social media trend, they are actually deeply researched psychological phenomena that come out of the attachment theory introduced by psychoanalyst John Bowlby in the 1950s, and expanded upon by developmental psychologist Mary Ainsworth in the 1960s and 1970s. It's a psychological framework that posits that early relationships with caregivers can shape an individual's emotional and social development, causing them to develop different attachment styles in relationships.

The four attachment styles are:

- **Anxious attachment**: characterized by clinginess and anxiety about being abandoned.
- **Avoidant attachment**: characterized by emotional distance and a reluctance to cede independence or depend upon others.
- **Disorganized attachment**: a mix of both behaviors above, rooted in trauma or inconsistent caregiving as a child.
- **Secure attachment**: characterized by security, trust, and safety in relationships.

Anxiously attached individuals can contribute to a lack of emotional security in the relationship by letting their anxieties run rampant. Those who are anxiously attached are needy, they seek constant reassurance, overanalyze everything, and have outsized reactions to setbacks and criticism. Clearly, these behaviors do not create a foundation of emotional security. These individuals often come off as fragile, hyper-sensitive, and prone to projection. This can make it difficult for their partner to feel emotionally secure enough to bring up problems in the relationship or to set boundaries, out of fear that their anxiously attached partner will fly off the handle, become distraught, or even have a total meltdown that will derail the conversation. Now, instead of discussing their partner's feelings, the anxiously attached person's emotions have taken center stage, and subsequently everything is focused on calming them down and reassuring them that the relationship is not about to end. In this instance, one person's emotions take massive precedence over the other's, and the non-anxiously attached partner will be left feeling as if they can never express themselves or get their needs met without the conversation being hijacked by their anxiously attached partner's needs.

On the opposite end of the spectrum, we have the avoidantly attached partner. This partner also creates emotional insecurity by shutting down at the slightest hint of difficulty in a relationship. These partners have difficulty establishing emotional intimacy and withdraw when someone tries to get close. They're uncomfortable not only with their own emotions, but with the emotions of others, and have difficulty expressing how they feel. Their defense mechanism encourages them to put up walls or flee the moment things get tough, leaving their partner to feel as if they can never bring up their own feelings or needs without risking abandonment. Avoidantly attached individuals will do anything to get away from feelings that they see as "negative," and will try to shut down any conversation involving negative emotions as "complaining." The problem is, true partnership means that sometimes people are going to complain. Negative emotions will arise, and partners should feel comfortable expressing those emotions to one another. Once again, we see an example of a relationship in which one person's comfort takes precedence over the other's feelings, leading to a situation where one partner feels as though they must constantly pretend everything is okay lest their partner decide to up and leave.

Finally, we have the rarest of all the attachment styles—the disorganized attachment style, which can feel like emotional whiplash to a partner. This attachment style manifests in constant vacillation between a need for closeness and a desire for distance. Someone with disorganized attachment may pursue a romantic relationship intensely at the beginning, only to withdraw as soon as the relationship gets closer. These individuals live in the extremes, often giving in to irrationality, selfishness, and suspicion. Partners of someone with

> THINK OF THIS AS THE CONCEPT OF GIVING YOUR PARTNER A "SAFE PLACE TO LAND."

a disorganized attachment style have no idea if broaching a difficult topic will cause their partner to fly off the handle or shut down. In this instance, one partner is constantly on their toes, never knowing what to expect from the other. In many ways, this is the ultimate lack of emotional security because one partner is left never knowing what to expect. As a result, they are constantly walking on eggshells, forever uncertain of how their partner will respond to challenges in the relationship.

Simply put, none of these three attachment styles lend themselves to emotionally secure relationships, and none are a fair way to treat someone who loves and cares about you.

There is hope, however! Much like the love languages, our attachment styles are not set in stone. Even though they are rooted in issues dating all the way back to our earliest moments of development, our attachment styles can be changed. Ultimately, we should all be working toward a secure attachment style, which anyone can achieve through a mix of therapy, self-reflection, and work with their partner. This takes a lot of effort and can be a lifelong project with ups and downs, leaps forward, and setbacks. Nobody is perfect, but once we actively engage in the attempt to create a more secure attachment style, a more emotionally secure relationship will follow.

EMOTIONALLY SECURE CONVERSATIONS

An emotionally secure conversation is one in which both parties find that they can express their feelings without fear of the other person's response. This doesn't mean that the other person is going to necessarily agree with everything that's being said. It just means that their partner knows that they can say it and be heard in a respectful manner that doesn't risk the end of the relationship or an emotional meltdown.

So, what does an emotionally secure conversation look like? They can take many forms. For example:

PARTNER A: *"I'm feeling really hurt that you stayed out until 3 a.m. last night and never responded to any of my texts. I get worried for your safety when you're gone for that long and I can't get in touch."*

PARTNER B: *"I understand where you're coming from. I like being able to have a late night out with friends from time to time and will continue to do so, but I'll make sure to check in with you more regularly so that you don't have to worry."*

In this example, Partner A was able to express how Partner B's actions made them feel, without being accusatory or making an unfair demand on their behavior (i.e., "You're not allowed to stay out late with your friends"). In response, Partner B listened to what Partner A had to say, established a boundary of their own (i.e., "Late nights out with friends are an important part of my social life"), and made a concession that acknowledged their partner's feelings but still allowed them to engage in social activities that are meaningful to them.

While it may have been tough for Partner A to bring up these feelings with Partner B due to their own anxieties and vulnerabilities, Partner B's response showed Partner A that these types of conversations won't lead to prolonged arguments, personal attacks, or hysterics. Now both partners know that they can talk about their feelings with one another without fear. *That's* what emotional security looks like. It doesn't mean no one will ever feel fear, hurt, sadness, or anger. It simply means that the emotions at play will never supersede the respect and love each partner has for the other, even when it's particularly difficult.

Here's another example of a highly emotionally sensitive conversation that is made better by emotional security:

PARTNER A: *"Hey love, I know this may be tough to hear, but I've been noticing that your hygiene habits have been falling behind. To be totally honest, it's affecting me, and I would hate to hear it's affecting your other relationships outside our home as well. Is something going on? If so, I want to be there for you and help you get back on track."*

PARTNER B: *"Ouch. Yeah, that's definitely tough to hear. To be honest, I've been feeling depressed and overwhelmed lately, and it's been making me less attentive to things like showering and brushing my teeth. I'm definitely feeling embarrassed right now, so I'm going to take a second with what you said before I decide on the best way you can support me."*

Telling someone they stink—for lack of a better phrase—stinks. In fact, it's one of the most emotionally fraught conversations two people can have. Yet, in a truly loving and emotionally secure relationship, even a topic as sensitive as body odor (I'm honestly cringing even thinking about this right now) should be on the table for discussion. In this example, Partner A started out with kindness and empathy, acknowledging that the topic was sensitive while also being honest about how it affects them. Most crucially, they opened up the floor for Partner B to say how they're feeling in return, as changes to hygiene habits can often be a sign of underlying emotional issues that go way deeper than a smelly armpit. In return, Partner B received the embarrassing information with grace and was honest about how the conversation made them feel.

Crucially, Partner B recognized that they were feeling strong emotions in response to the conversation and decided to step away for a few moments so that they could work through some of the anger and defensiveness they may have been feeling on their own. There's nothing wrong with honoring your anger. In fact, learning how to do so in a mature way is one of the most vital aspects of creating an emotionally secure relationship for all parties involved.

EMOTIONALLY SECURE ANGER

You may be reading all of this and thinking, "That sounds all well and good, but what about when I'm feeling really, *really* pissed." And reader, you're not alone. Anger is an emotion that many people struggle with expressing in an emotionally secure way. And by "many people," I mean myself.

Yep, that's right. I struggle with expressing anger in my relationships. My therapist calls these out-of-control moments of rage "emotional dysregulation," and they were a major hurdle that I had to overcome in order to be a better partner, friend, family member, and human being. Not only was my inability to stay in control when I felt anger affecting my ability to show love to the people closest to me, it affected my ability to show love to myself. When you let your anger take the wheel in a dysregulated, emotionally insecure way, you come

> ANGER IS AN EMOTION THAT MANY PEOPLE STRUGGLE WITH EXPRESSING IN AN EMOTIONALLY SECURE WAY.

out the other side feeling drained, wounded, and ashamed.

Getting control of my anger wasn't just something that I needed to do for myself. It was something that I needed to do for my marriage, and my dreams of having a family in the future. The fact of the matter was, when I was at my worst with anger and emotional dysregulation, I was not a safe person to be around. After years of letting my anger and emotionality get the best of me, I knew that I had to do some serious work if I wanted to be the type of person a partner or child would ever see as a safe space.

After a lot of personal work and growth, I still know I'm never going to be someone who isn't emotionally vulnerable. In fact, I've learned that my emotional vulnerability and sensitivity—when properly managed—is a strength that helps me engage with the world in an open and empathetic way. The point of managing my emotions isn't for me to remove all emotional vulnerability from my life, it's to make sure that that vulnerability doesn't control my life, and in doing so create more emotional security for myself and my partners.

Being a highly emotional person is not something you need to be ashamed of. In fact, it often means you

have a high level of empathy, sense of justice, and are observant about the world around you. The catch is, you can't let your emotions run the show, and you need to make sure that you're still creating an emotionally secure environment where your partner feels that they can also express themselves.

So, what do we do when we start seeing red and know that our anger is itching to take the wheel and send us careening off the emotional-security cliff? Here are just a few strategies that have worked for me, but know that there are many strategies that us sensitive Sallys can use to stay grounded, even when on the edge of losing control.

- **Step away from the conversation.** Full disclosure, I really struggle with this, but I've come to learn its value. Go into a different room. Take a walk around the block. Do whatever it takes to separate yourself from your partner, while you allow the first wave of ultra-heightened emotions to pass.

- **Deep breaths.** This suggestion is so obvious, you may even roll your eyes at my bringing it up here, but nothing reconnects you to your body and your peace like a breathing exercise. There are tons of different exercises you can try in order to find the one that best calms you down. Personally, I like box breathing, which involves inhaling slowly through your nostrils for a count of four, holding your breath for a count of four, exhaling for a count of four, holding your breath for a count of four, and then starting again. It really works! Plus, it's nearly imperceptible to others, so you can box breathe anywhere—even during a work meeting that you're 100 percent sure could have been an email.

- **Scream into a pillow.** Sometimes you just have to release the steam valve and let it all out. While screaming at your partner can leave them feeling frightened or traumatized, a pillow has none of those emotions! In moments

of intense anger, walk into another room (stepping away ftw!), grab a pillow or cushion, put it to your face, and just really let loose. The pillow won't mind, and neither will your neighbors.

- **Shock your system with something cold.** This may seem extreme, but it really works. Sometimes in moments of intense anger, our bodies really need a nervous system reset. Grabbing onto some ice cubes, a cooling eye mask, or even hopping into a cold shower can do the trick. The biggest hurdle with this strategy is ego, a.k.a. the desire not to seem "crazy" while you engage in your own mini ice-bucket challenge to calm down. But you know what's crazier? Not using a free strategy that is scientifically proven to work just because you're afraid of how it looks to other people. In fact, in an emotionally secure relationship, your partner should understand and respect your need for an unconventional method of calming yourself down. Emotional security goes both ways, after all.

> SOMETIMES YOU JUST HAVE TO RELEASE THE STEAM VALVE AND LET IT ALL OUT.

As I said, these are just a few of an almost infinite number of strategies you can use to turn down the heat on your anger, and establish more emotional security in your life. The point isn't to avoid feeling anger or to never express it. The point is to make sure that even when you do, you're still leading with love, respect, and stability above all else.

You can disagree strongly with what your partner is saying, or how to proceed on critical issues such as finances or parenting, while still providing emotional security. Which sets us up perfectly for our next new love language for the modern era. It's funny how we keep doing that, huh?

HEALTHY DEBATE

This new love language is similar to emotional security, but with its own unique twist. Introducing . . . healthy debate! The principle behind this is simple: partners should be able to disagree with each other respectfully about things such as movies, television, books, or even take different sides on the latest drama in your friendship group without nastiness or hostility from the other side. Healthy debate is always built on a foundation of love because it conveys to your partner, "I love you, even if I hate your taste in scented candles."

A partnership is a negotiation, and differences of opinion are going to come up. In a healthy debate, everyone involved is given time to explain their point of view. While one partner is talking, the other isn't constantly interrupting, rolling their eyes, or simply waiting for their time to jump in with a monologue. In a healthy debate, both sides *actually listen* while the other person is talking, and genuinely take time to consider the merit of what the other person is saying, or even that they could be right. (Although often there will be no objective "right" or "wrong" in these discussions.) A healthy debate means a conversation where:

- **Nobody resorts to personal attacks to make their point.**
- **Everyone involved uses a respectful tone (no raised voices, no sarcasm, no condescension).**
- **Everyone gets a chance to talk and express their point of view.**
- **Each partner is open to what the other has to say.**

When you follow these simple rules of engagement, debate can not only be healthy, but also fun and intellectually stimulating. Debates that start from a foundation of respect can often bring the debaters closer together as sparring partners and "worthy opponents." In fact, those who debate academically, or professionally, will often say that the only way to win is to not only see and understand your side, but to see and understand the side of your opponent.

In a respectful debate, both sides see the other as intellectual equals, whose ideas are worthy of being discussed and deconstructed.

There are, of course, key differences when we're talking about a debate between partners and a debate that takes place in an academic setting, which includes judges and an explicit ability to win or lose. In a healthy debate between two partners, your goal shouldn't be to "take down" the other person or to "win" the argument in the way it would be if you were debating someone from a rival school.

OK, so you can want to win a *little*. We're all human. But the desire to "win" the debate should never supersede the desire to show respect to the person you're debating. Your goal during a healthy debate should simply be to express yourself in a way that makes you feel as if your thoughts have been well represented, and to allow your partner to do the same. If things start to get heated, staying committed to healthy debate may mean that you and your partner agree to step away from the conversation for a time, drop the subject, or simply "agree to disagree" on the issue for the time being. Sometimes the healthiest resolution to a debate is to realize that you and your partner feel differently about a subject and that's not going to change.

HEALTHY DEBATE IN THE MODERN ERA

Don't worry, reader. I can already hear you asking the question that is at the forefront of everyone's mind when the topic of healthy debate between partners comes up: *but what about politics?*

We live in an intensely political and divided time, where some of our most important values, from women's rights to racial equality to environmental protections, are constantly being brought up for public debates that can be upsetting and exhausting to witness from the sidelines. So, it should come as no surprise that, for many people, engaging in those debates at home is a nonstarter. In fact, living in a home where fundamental values aren't agreed upon can lead to an erosion of emotional security and negative mental-health outcomes.

> HEALTHY DEBATE IN A RELATIONSHIP DOESN'T MEAN THAT YOU SHOULD BE OKAY WITH ANY OPINION YOUR PARTNER MAY EXPRESS.

Everyone has certain core values that they need their partners to be aligned with in order to have a successful partnership. Sometimes, these core values show up in the form of boundaries (see how all these love languages tie in together?), and placing a boundary on what political views you can or cannot differ on with a partner is not a failure of open mindedness. Ignoring your own values in service of being open minded or allowing for endless, exhausting debates is not actually healthy, and it's not what we're talking about here.

Of course, that doesn't mean you can't make a partnership work with someone whose views don't exactly align with yours. In fact, when it comes to political differences, it is highly unlikely that two (or more!) people are going to have the exact same views on every political issue for all of their time together. Indeed, you and your partner may have serious differences about specific policies, politicians, laws, or ways of approaching political activism. However, being committed to healthy debate with your partner doesn't mean you need to "agree to disagree" on issues related to your core values such as anti-racism, rejecting homophobia, or supporting civil rights for women and other marginalized groups. Healthy debate in a relationship doesn't mean that you should be OK with any opinion your partner may express, or that finding out your partner's opinion on an issue that matters to you can't change your opinion of them in turn. If you don't want to enter into a romantic partnership with someone who votes for a certain political party or politician because you see that vote as an expression of a fundamental difference in your core values, that's a valid boundary to put in place.

Healthy debate doesn't mean that you and your partner can disagree on any topic without consequence. It just means that when you and your partner are debating an issue that you both view differently, you can do so in a respectful way. This means both sides are allowed to share their thoughts, stand their ground, and make their own decisions while still feeling respected and heard.

BETTER DEBATING STRATEGIES

A healthy debate should be looked at, in essence, as a negotiation instead of a fight. In a long-term partnership, the chances are you're going to find yourself and your partner debating

and negotiating on all sorts of topics. There are the small, day-to-day debates, such as where to eat out on a Saturday night (your old favorite or the new place that just opened up down the street?). Then, there will be debates about big life decisions, such as where to move next, how to allocate your joint finances, and whether or not it's time to adopt a puppy (the answer to this last one is always yes, by the way). There will also be philosophical debates, in which you may find that you and your partner have different views on abstract questions, such as what constitutes a white lie, what makes a good friend, or even the nature of good and evil. There will be debates about art. There will be debates about culture. There will be debates about people and social situations, and even about whether or not you'd still love each other if one of you had been turned into a worm. (We can thank TikTok for that final deeply philosophical question.)

So, how do we ensure that these debates don't move from playful intellectual sparring to hurtful attacks? Here are five better debating strategies you can employ next time you and your partner find yourselves on opposing sides of an argument.

- **Acknowledge feelings**. Try to really hear what your partner is saying about how the debate makes them feel, and what is fueling their strong opinion on the subject.

- **Be curious.** Try to approach the debate from a place of sincere curiosity about why your partner feels the way they feel and ask genuine questions to learn more.

- **Use an "I" statement**. When you're explaining your point of view, focus on yourself. Use statements that center on your own experience and feelings, rather than "you" statements that assume your partner's motives or thoughts, and can sound accusatory, condescending, or both.

TRY TO REALLY HEAR WHAT YOUR PARTNER IS SAYING ABOUT HOW THE DEBATE MAKES THEM FEEL, AND WHAT IS FUELING THEIR STRONG OPINION.

- **Be willing to be wrong.** Have an open mind! You know your partner to be a smart, thoughtful person (if not, that's a whole other discussion), so perhaps they're right? Stranger things have happened . . .

- **Don't be a jerk.** If you're only going to focus on one of the suggestions on this list, this is the one. Debate your partner from a place of respect. Don't be condescending, rude, pedantic, or hurtful. Again, the goal of a debate with your partner shouldn't be to win, it should be to remain loving and respectful—otherwise, everyone loses.

Alright, reader. We've talked a lot about how to deal with differences since introducing our new love languages. Now it's time to talk about a new love language based entirely on what you and your partner share.

SHARED GOALS & EXPERIENCES

The last three new love languages that we've proposed are centered around conflict and conflict resolution because how we deal with friction in a partnership sets the tone for how we deal with everything else. However, I sincerely hope that conflict isn't the majority of your relationship. (And if it is . . . you might want to think about that.)

So, what *should* the majority of your relationship be? Enter our next love language for the modern era—shared goals and experiences! What is a first date, if not an opportunity to suss out whether the other person has similar interests, goals, and hobbies to you? (And to make sure they actually look like their profile photo, of course.) The fact of the matter is, the further down the relationship road you and your partner go, the more time you're going to spend together. This doesn't just mean big-ticket activities such as vacations and holidays, but everyday moments, such as watching TV together, taking your cat to the vet, or simply falling asleep side by side.

The best partnerships are the ones where everyone involved feels as if they are invested in each other's lives. This means being a cheerleader for goals both big and small, and seeking out opportunities to achieve shared goals together. These goals can be financial (saving for a house), personal (learning a new language together), or project-based (redecorating/renovating a room, building a new piece of furniture, etc.). The point is for you both to be invested and work toward something together.

Shared experiences represent the joy of being in a partnership with someone else. They're foundational experiences that you can both come back to, even if you're going through a rough patch, to remind yourselves of the love you've cultivated and all the beautiful things your partnership has brought to your lives. There's a reason why "We'll always have Paris," is one of the most famous lines in *Casablanca* (a movie known for its iconic lines): it speaks to the universal experience of sharing something so special and life changing with someone that it will always tie you together, even when you're far apart. It's the reason why many couples have fond memories of times long gone, when they were young, struggling financially, and figuring out where they wanted to go in life. My own parents will often wax lyrical about the year they moved across the country, lived in a tiny Los Angeles apartment, and slept on old lounge chairs instead of a bed while they looked for jobs. The faraway look in their eyes while they talk about these times isn't because they long to return to the lounge chairs—I don't think my dad's back could handle it these days—but because it's something they went through together, and their partnership was strengthened as a result.

Shared goals work in much the same way. Joy is best when it's shared. When a couple sets out to save up for a house and finally get the keys, their joy is compounded because they did it together. But it's not just the joy that's shared: sharing a goal with someone else means that you get to share the frustrations, the hardships, the ups and downs of getting to the end. It means when you finally achieve what you set out to do, there's someone else there who fully understands what it took for you to get there. In the unfortunate event that your goal is not reached, it means that there's someone else there to share in the pain, understand the loss, and help you work through the emotions as you move on to your next great adventure.

SHARED EXPERIENCES

You and your partner are unlikely to love the exact same things—opposites do attract, after all—but you should share *some* activities that you both find equally enjoyable, and be open and interested in the ones that you don't. In my own marriage, I love gardening, my husband loves football, and neither of us knew a goddamn thing about the other. Yet, because I respect my husband and his interests, I now know a lot more about football than I did before we got together. I know the players on his favorite team, the Green Bay Packers (Go Pack Go!). I know what game he is watching and what he hopes the outcome will be, and when Super Bowl season comes around, I can sit and watch the game with him and enjoy it, even if I'm still not 100 percent sure how the game is played. In return, my husband listens to me excitedly gush over my garden. I can tell him about how our pole beans are doing (very well, by the way) and all about my plans for what to grow next season. When my attempt to grow a pumpkin on our rooftop deck failed spectacularly due to one of New York's classic summer heatwaves, he lent a sympathetic ear to my disappointment. The gardening itself may not have been a shared experience, but through his listening and interest, I still felt supported and understood in my passion. (And I'll make that pumpkin happen next year . . . I swear.)

So, what about *truly* shared experiences—the ones that both of you are fully invested in from start to finish? These moments are powerful fuel for love, respect, and stability in a relationship that can sustain you even through the most difficult times. (Which can, in turn, become shared experiences themselves. It's funny how that works, isn't it?)

Shared experiences can be big or small. Parenthood is a major shared experience that can make or break a partnership. Those who are able to work together to build their new family—and laugh at the occasional diaper blowout—will come out stronger in the long run. Those who refuse to share the burden, selfishly leaving one partner to do all the work in isolation, will put an insurmountable wedge between themselves, as one partner moves forward into parenthood and the other remains in the past. It is that shared experience of raising a child that turns partners into parents, not the presence of a baby.

Other major life events can also be shared experiences—from vacations to moves, to growing old, and loss. Sharing in life's most precious moments helps to bring couples together in new ways. No one forgets who was by their side when their mother passed away, and the simple deed of standing by someone's side to share in their pain is one of the most powerful acts of love there is.

But enough about death and dying! Like I said, shared experiences are also the *fun* part of a relationship. One of my favorite ways to create shared experiences with my husband is on vacation. Some of our cherished stories from our relationship took place on vacation—from a marijuana dispensary tour gone wrong in Denver to a treasured trip we took to perform comedy in Berlin. Two years later, we built even more treasured memories on our honeymoon, a two-week-long road trip across the southwestern USA. In the years since, we'll often look

> SHARING IN LIFE'S MOST PRECIOUS MOMENTS HELPS TO BRING COUPLES TOGETHER IN NEW WAYS.

back on the country music we listened to while on the road, the strange and hilarious characters we met in Las Vegas, and the awe we both felt looking at the Grand Canyon for the first time, as moments of shared joy that have since become core to the story of our relationship. These trips weren't just fun vacations, they were foundational experiences of love that we come back to again and again.

You may get the impression from what I'm saying that shared experiences need to be grand, expensive gestures, but that's not true at all. The point of shared experiences is simply that they are shared. Shared experiences can also be small moments of joy and discovery. In fact, it's probably the small shared experiences that are accumulated over time that matter most. A beautiful day in the park, seeing a highly anticipated movie in theaters and talking about it afterward, going for a walk in your neighborhood, or even just a lazy Sunday spent at home binge-watching your favorite trashy reality TV show, are all building blocks to greater connection. These are the moments from which inside jokes are born (like yelling "A new bombshell has entered the villa!" any time our cat comes out from her hiding spot under the bed) and each little moment is a stepping stone to learning more about each other and building a stronger relationship—brick by brick, laugh by laugh, experience by experience.

Here are four key types of shared experiences that might help cement your relationship:

- **Milestone moments.** A powerful bond is formed when someone sees you through different life phases. Life experiences are all about shared milestone moments, from becoming parents to losing parents to making your first million.

- **Date nights and late nights.** These are the vacations, the projects, the nights out with friends, and the nights in with a bottle of wine that made you want to be in your partnership in the first place. They're the things that you and your partner love doing together that fill your shared well of happiness.

- **First-time experiences.** These can be anything from trying an adventurous new cuisine to the birth of your first child. The point is that when you and your partner

> THE POINT OF SHARED EXPERIENCES IS SIMPLY THAT THEY ARE SHARED.

experience something together for the first time, a deeper bond is formed as you learn and grow together as a couple.

- **Moments of joy.** These shared experiences are the little things. They're the funny thing you saw while out on a walk, the way the sunset looks coming through your bedroom window, the cute way your dog rolls around on the carpet after a bath. They're small moments of happiness that, over time, make a huge impact.

Ideally, your relationship would be a perfect blend of these different types of shared experiences at all times. In reality, it can be hard to bring them all into balance. For example, a new parent's life is full of milestone moments, first-time experiences, and moments of joy, but they may be *severely* lacking in the date nights and late nights category. If you're feeling that your relationship is stuck in a rut, it could be that you haven't had one of these types of shared experiences for a while, or you need to spend a little more time keeping an eye out for your moments of joy.

SHARED GOALS

You really can't have a functional partnership without shared goals. No matter how great your chemistry is or how much you enjoy each other's company, if you and your partner have totally different visions for what a happy life together will look like, it's just not going to work. Just think about some classic first date questions:

- "What do you do for fun?"
- "Where do you see yourself in five years?"
- "What's your family like?"
- "What's your sign?"

They may seem cliché, but they're all getting at the same thing: do we have compatible views on what a happy life will be? There are plenty of people who may enjoy each other's company immensely but wouldn't make good partners because they have fundamentally different goals for their lives. I see this all the time in advice columns (here I go again about my beloved advice columns . . .) around the issue of whether or not to have children. It's a sad but familiar story—one partner wants to have kids and the other does not. They love each other. They get along great. They've already built a bedrock of shared experiences that they both treasure. But at the end of the day, no one has the right to force another person into or out of parenthood if that's what they want for their life. If they try, the partner forced to give up their dream of being a parent may feel resentful and empty, always wondering what could have been, if their partner had just relented on the issue of kids. On the flip side, a person with no desire to be a parent who only became one to appease their partner may also end up feeling resentful, always wondering what adventures they may have had, if they didn't have to be responsible for the wellbeing of a child. Many otherwise happy partnerships break up over this issue, knowing that the sadness that will come down the line will erode any happiness that they share now.

Here I am going on about sadness again when the point of this love language is really to share in joy! Why do I keep doing that? Something to bring up with my therapist, for sure.

Much like shared experiences, shared goals can be big or small, expensive or totally free. Some examples of small shared goals could be:

- Joining a running club together or training for a marathon.
- House training your new puppy.
- Setting aside a day to deep clean your apartment (which reminds me—my husband and I really need to set aside a day to deep clean our apartment).
- Maintaining your houseplants.
- Painting your bedroom a new color that you both love.
- Learning a new language together (or any new skill, really!)
- Watching every Academy Award Best Picture nominee for the year.
- Checking out all the best hiking spots in your area.

The list goes on and on! The point of small, shared goals is to make sure that you and your partner always have something to work toward that is equally meaningful to you both. They're little things that you do daily, weekly, or monthly that help bring you together through a sense of accomplishment and allow you to build a shared language of joy.

Larger shared goals do all of that and more. These are the goals that may take months, years, or even a lifetime to accomplish. They're the goals that you create as part of your shared mission to build a life you desire together. When they're accomplished, your connection deepens, not just through the shared sense of accomplishment, but also through the celebration of a hard-fought goal finally made reality. (Because yes, you should totally find a way to celebrate when you accomplish one of these big-ticket goals).

Many shared goals and experiences go hand-in-hand. As we've already discussed, parenthood is a common large, shared goal for romantic partners. For some, this goal is easily achieved, while for others, it's a hard-fought battle that is a shared experience in and of itself. This initial goal of becoming parents will give way to an avalanche of other goals that you will now create together as you decide what's best for your child.

Along the way, the shared experience of parenthood will act as a powerful bonding agent for you and your partner as you learn about yourselves as parents and are introduced to the tiny, independent human that you both worked together to create.

However, parenthood isn't the only large, shared goal romantic partners can have. In fact, the decision not to become parents creates the shared experience of navigating the world as childfree adults.

Some examples of larger shared goals include:

- Saving for a house.
- Saving for retirement.
- Finally booking that trip around the world.
- Planning a wedding.
- Making a cross-country move.
- Starting a new business.
- Renovating your home.

As you can see, many of the larger shared goals you'll create as a couple are linked with the life events you'll go through together. Much like shared experiences, these moments signify that you and your partner are entering into a new phase of life side-by-side, hand-in-hand. Many of these goals can be financial, but they don't have to be. Goals can also be centered around health, spirituality, emotional wellness, and your own relationship.

One shared goal should be to build a partnership based on love and respect. This means striving for things such as better communication, greater intimacy, and deeper understanding of each other's internal selves, that will span your entire relationship. They're not goals you'll be able to get the satisfaction of checking off a to-do list (because is there any greater satisfaction than checking something off a to-do list?) such as saving for a house or booking that dream holiday, but they serve as joint motivation for you and your loved one to be better to each other.

Some examples of loving relationship goals include:

- Improving your communication with one another.
- Improving your sex life.
- Acting as a team.
- Building a loving home.

SHARING PERSONAL GOALS

Sometimes, a personal goal can become a shared goal if sacrifices are required from both parties to make it happen. Just think about all the Academy Award winners who say they share their award with their partners in their acceptance speech—they're not just saying it to be nice. It's likely that the actor was away from home for months—potentially years—working on their film, leaving their partner behind

to run the household and deal with the loneliness that comes from being in a long-distance relationship. Perhaps their partner also helped run lines with them, dropped everything to help with a last-minute audition, and supported their partner through the many ups and downs of life as a working actor. They were an integral part of helping their partner achieve their dream, and so they truly do share in that award. I hear a similar refrain from doctors whose partners supported them through medical school and residency, when long hours made them less available both emotionally and physically.

Part of being a true partner to someone is being a cheerleader for their personal goals. This should be something you do for each other freely and fairly. By "fairly," I mean that both partners' life goals should carry the same level of weight in the relationship. The partner who stood by their actor spouse on their way to Oscar-winning glory should be able to ask for the same support when they want to start a new business, or go back to school. The partner who sacrificed intimacy while their spouse was in medical school should be able to ask to refocus on their relationship goals now that those personal goals have been met. In relationships where one person's goals are always prioritized over the other, or where personal goals always take precedence over goals for the relationship, partners can find that they've forgotten how to speak this very crucial love language.

> PART OF BEING A TRUE PARTNER IS BEING A CHEERLEADER FOR THEIR PERSONAL GOALS.

I've said it once and I'll say it again: joy is best when shared. With this final new love language, shared joy is a springboard for building a life of happiness and deeper connection with your partner.

QUIZ

NEW ROMANTIC LOVE LANGUAGES

And now, the moment you've all been waiting for . . . your first quiz! Now that we've introduced four new love languages, it's time for you to figure out which of these ranks highest on your menu of love. As a reminder, you'll need to speak a little bit of all these love languages to truly create a partnership built on love and respect, but it never hurts to know which language you speak more fluently than others.

Read each of the following statements and circle the answer that best describes you, then turn to page 156 to discover your Romantic Love Languages preferences.

D I feel most respected when my partner gives me the space I ask for.

B I feel most respected when my partner lets me say my piece.

A I feel most connected to my partner when we try something new together.

C I feel most connected to my partner when we get through something hard together.

B I always notice when my partner listens.

D I always notice when my partner does what I ask.

B In arguments, it is most meaningful to me to be heard.

C In arguments, it is most meaningful to me to be calm.

D A good partner is someone who is willing to make sacrifices.

A A good partner is someone who is up for anything.

C A good partner is a good listener.

B A good partner is a good communicator.

A I love to go out with my partner.

C I love to stay in with my partner.

B Communication is key to a healthy relationship.

A Joy is key to a healthy relationship.

D Respect is key to a healthy relationship.

C Security is key to a healthy relationship.

D I want a partner who understands my history.

A I want a partner who understands my heart.

PART TWO:

LOVE LESSONS BEYOND ROMANCE

Romantic love is great, but we know that's not all there is. From family to friends, to the coworkers who keep us sane and the neighbors who always lend a helping hand, there are so many people in the world who are worthy of our love. So how do we apply the love languages to those relationships? In this section, we'll talk about how to do just that!

LOVE LANGUAGES & PLATONIC LOVE

When people talk about the five love languages, they're generally talking about romantic love—and with good reason! That was the focus of Chapman's original book, and that's where we started with our book as well. But, as we take a more expansive view of the love languages, it's important that we expand our definition of love to include all of its forms. To continue with our "menu of love" metaphor, romantic love is just one of many flavors that love can come in. Humanity is blessed to be able to share love in ways that go well beyond the romantic, from the love between family members, to love between friends, to the love that is shared between all people, broadly, just for being human. (Yes, even your coworkers.)

In this section of the book, we're going to dive a little bit deeper into how the love languages fit into our platonic relationships. Each of the original five love languages and the four new love languages that we've added, are applicable well beyond our romantic relationships. In general, someone who thinks of themselves as a gift-giver is a gift-giver in all sorts of situations—from anniversaries with their partners to the holiday gift exchange in the office. Someone who is physically affectionate with their lovers is also likely to be physically affectionate with their family and friends (albeit in a different way). Someone who values quality time with their partner will likely value quality time with their BFF. Someone who appreciates words of affirmation or acts of service will appreciate them from friends, family, and mentors alike, and so on and so forth.

Filling your life with platonic love has enormous benefits—these relationships are often where we go to seek guidance, blow off steam, or get reassurance when our romantic relationships are either non-existent or in crisis. In society, we sometimes see romantic love held above all others as necessary for a happy, fulfilled life: the princess can't live "happily ever after" without her prince, after all. Yet, in real life, we can see that this laser focus on romantic love above the powerful bonds of friendship, family, and other forms of human connection, can be to our detriment. Who's to say that the single person who spends their days cultivating lifelong friendships has less love in their life than someone who has a romantic partner? Or that the aunt who dotes on her nieces and nephews is somehow unsatisfied because she doesn't have children of her own? This way of thinking is outdated, and is increasingly being replaced with new, fresh ideas about the ways in which love and human connection can be expressed outside a romantic partnership.

This goes well beyond the people we are "supposed" to love, such as our friends and family. Love is an expansive emotion, and we humans are able to give and receive it with just about anyone. Even in the workplace, where norms around professionalism dictate our behavior, we can still express love in appropriate ways that will help foster more respect between coworkers and—frankly—make the office an overall better place to spend time.

So, how do we use love languages to express love in our platonic relationships? Let's start with some of the people in our lives who are easiest to love—our friends.

LOVE LANGUAGES & FRIENDSHIP

Bestie. BFF. Ride-or-die. These are just a few of the hundreds of ways we humans have come up with to describe the people who make some of the biggest impacts on our lives. They may not be someone we kiss or sleep with. They may not share a relative with us. But, they've made an impression on our lives and we know they deserve a special designation.

They are our friends, and making sure our friendships remain loving, happy, and healthy is one of the most universally agreed upon ways to live a long and fulfilling life. A 2023 study published in the Cambridge University Press looked at the friendships of nearly 13,000 fifty-year-olds and found that not only did maintaining strong friendships correlate with reduced rates of depression and stroke, but it also correlated with a longer lifespan. Some studies have even found that individuals with a strong social network are less likely to die *of all causes*. Friends aren't just great to have because they'll show up with a bottle of wine after a breakup or text to make sure we got home okay after a night out. They literally keep us healthy, and love languages are a great tool for expressing how much these special relationships mean to us.

You would think that in a time of increased connectivity through the internet and social media people would be feeling less isolated, but it turns out the opposite is true. It's been five years since the UK appointed its first ministerial lead for loneliness (sometimes referred to as their "Minister for Loneliness") to investigate how to reduce loneliness in the country. In the USA, former surgeon general Vivek Murthy has been sounding the alarm about increased loneliness since 2020, even going so far as to call loneliness an "epidemic" in need of urgent attention. All over the world, the effects of isolation and loneliness are taking their toll. It seems

that the ability to "keep up" with our friends by liking each other's selfies or DMing the occasional meme, is a poor substitute for genuine connection.

Of course, I'm not saying you should stop liking your friends' selfies or sending them memes (after all, what is that little heart you double tap supposed to be if not its own mini expression of love?) but clearly, something more is needed. Luckily, we have our new and improved menu of love to help us show our friends we care and deepen our connections. Much like in our romantic relationships, applying the love languages to your friendships means not only investigating the ways you like to receive love, but also paying close attention to how your friends like to receive love, and how, as with romantic love, this can change depending on the circumstances. Speaking to a friend in their preferred love language is just another way to show them that you see them and accept them as they are. It communicates that their feelings and comfort are important to you, and that you know them well enough to know gift exchanges give them anxiety or the exact right words of affirmation they need to hear after a bad day at work. These gestures may seem simple, but sometimes it's the small things we do for each other that truly make a difference.

FRIENDSHIP & WORDS OF AFFIRMATION

Do you tell your friends you love them? Seriously, do you say the words "I love you." If not, incorporating more words of affirmation into your friendship can start right there. Unlike in romantic relationships, where saying "I love you" for the first time carries with it the baggage of potential rejection and added commitment, we can freely express our love to friends without fear. Or at least, we *should* be able to freely express love to our friends without fear. For some reason, in our modern times, some of us feel a lot less comfortable effusively expressing admiration for our friends. This can especially affect heterosexual men. It was not long ago that letters between men would end with "affectionately yours" or address each other as "my lovely boy." Nowadays, ideas around traditional masculinity (which we can actually see is not traditional at all) and the strictures of patriarchy often hold our straight male friends back from expressing their full range of emotions, even something as joyful as love for a friend. One way to help break them out of this way of thinking is to show them love with words of affirmation. Not in the sense that you should shower or coddle them with unnecessary praise, but just the simple act of being honest with them about the fact that you enjoy their company, and explaining why, can crack open a door that begins to let their own emotions and words of affirmation flow.

Women are often much more effusive with their friendships. It's not uncommon for two women who just met in line for the bathroom to be throwing around "I love you" by the time they're washing their hands. In a society that often tells women they're too loud or not pretty enough, many have taken it upon themselves to hype each other up and provide the affirmations that society won't. Women will often freely compliment each other on the street, or leave encouraging comments on social media. This doesn't mean, however, that your friends may not still be struggling internally with self-worth, imposter syndrome, body dysmorphia, or a whole host of other insecurities that society encourages women to feel. Sometimes, we take it as a given that our friends know how funny, kind, intelligent, or beautiful they are. If they weren't all these things, why would you be friends with them? Yet, the truth is most of us don't fully realize all the wonderful things we bring to the table. That's why words of affirmation can be such a powerful tool when giving or receiving love as a friend. The implications of kind words from a friend are huge. Just think about it! Here's someone who isn't related to you, isn't romantically tied to you, and isn't under any obligation to spend time with you, willingly expressing that they enjoy having you in their life. Kind words from a friend show us all that we have someone in our corner, who is choosing to be there just because. In a world of increased loneliness and isolation, friendship is one of the most powerful forms of love we can offer one another.

During hard times, it's often the simple "I'm thinking of you" text that can mean the most when coming from a friend. Nothing made this more clear than the COVID-19 pandemic, when words of affirmation and encouragement were often the only things friends could offer one another. Although we were physically separated, friendships were maintained over text, video chat, letters, and care packages. As we all struggled to adjust to the new normal, words of affirmation helped us keep each other going by communicating a powerful message: we're all in this together.

DURING HARD TIMES, IT'S OFTEN THE SIMPLE "I'M THINKING OF YOU" TEXT THAT CAN MEAN THE MOST WHEN COMING FROM A FRIEND.

FRIENDSHIP & QUALITY TIME

It's hard to overstate the importance of making time for your friends. Our friends are often the people who know us best, and are there for us when romantic or familial relationships fall short. Even something as simple as catching up with a friend over coffee can leave us feeling more relaxed, and help us feel more connected to ourselves and the simple joys of life. There's just something about belly laughing to a decades-old inside joke that can chase any blues away, even just for a little while.

As we get older, making time for our friendships gets harder and

harder. Gone are the days of playdates orchestrated by mom and dad or mandatory hours spent sitting at desks side-by-side in school. Now work, kids, long distances, and the general exhaustion of being an adult can all get in the way of spending time with friends. Suddenly, a relationship that once seemed to maintain itself can take a lot of work and planning from both parties to keep afloat. Best friends who were once inseparable in their college years can end up in totally different parts of the country. As painful as this part of adulthood can be, friendships changing as we age are a fact of life. During these times, we may need to reframe what we think quality time looks like to make it through.

If anything good can be said about the COVID-19 pandemic, it's that it made us all much more adept at finding ways to spend time together without actually being together physically. Through video calls, Netflix watch parties, and online gaming, many of us were able to create new, virtual spaces for spending quality time together. While I think it's safe to say we're all happy to have in-person connections back on the table, there's no reason why we can't take what we learned during those dark days of lockdown and apply them to the times when our friendships may be harder to maintain.

The need to adjust how you spend quality time in a friendship is never so clear as when your friends start having kids. Suddenly, a friend who you could always count on for movie nights and coffee dates is trapped under a pile of diapers, and even when they do manage to escape, they're too exhausted to do anything but catch up on the sleep they haven't been getting since their little bundle of joy arrived. If you're a person with quality time as one of your preferred love languages, this can be an incredibly difficult period in a friendship. Many single or child-free people whose friends all have kids, report not only a lack of quality time with their friends but also a lack of quality conversation. New parents' brains are often (understandably) wired to be focused only on their new baby. They may forget to ask their child-free friend about their new job or creative projects. They may fail to show up for important events or even realize that months have passed since the last time you saw each other. If a friendship is going to survive this upheaval in the norm, it will be important for both friends to get on the same page about quality time.

For the child-free friend, this may be a time when they seek out in-person, regular quality time elsewhere, and with friends who are in a similar life phase. They may have to recognize that their standing Wednesday-night dinner date may no longer be able to happen, but it can shift to a Wednesday-night phone call instead. For the new-parent friend, it's important that they don't lose sight of maintaining their friendships entirely. True friends will understand that this is a busy time in their life, but nobody likes feeling like an afterthought, and even the most resilient succulent needs to be watered every once in a while. If you have to, set regular reminders to check in with your friends, either in person or virtually. When you do, don't forget to let some of your conversations focus on what's going on with them before you dive into your next harrowing diaper blowout story.

Friendships that truly stand the test of time are the ones that make allowances for the ebbs and flows of life. What quality time looks like in your teens will look different when you go away to college. Friends who were inseparable in college will have to adjust to seeing each other only a few times a year as people move away to pursue their dreams. On the flip side, friendships that faltered during the new-parent phase may very well blossom again when the kids get older, or when an unexpected move brings you closer together. By allowing expectations around quality time to ebb and flow with the friendship, you're allowing the friendship to grow and change and, ultimately, survive.

FRIENDSHIP & RECEIVING GIFTS

People's relationships with gifts and gift-giving can be complicated. What can be seen as the ultimate expression of love to one person can be nothing but an anxiety-inducing, empty ritual to others. For people who identify as gift-givers, thoughtless or forgotten

> FRIENDSHIPS THAT TRULY STAND THE TEST OF TIME ARE THE ONES THAT MAKE ALLOWANCES FOR THE EBBS AND FLOWS OF LIFE.

gifts can seem like the ultimate sign of disrespect. For those who experience what I like to call "gift anxiety," they'd love nothing more than to scrap all the gifting and focus on the other love languages instead. When two people on opposite ends of the gift-giving spectrum become friends, they'll need to both be careful to navigate their feelings around gift-giving in an open, honest way to avoid hurt feelings and misunderstandings.

So, how do you actually do that? By letting go. The gift-giving friend is still welcome to give gifts, but they should let go of the expectation that they'll receive similar gifts in return. Perhaps they can instead try to focus on the many other ways their friend shows up for them, and reframe those actions as gifts. They may not be the type of friend to always send a perfectly wrapped package for your birthday or who brings a little something from the gift shop after a trip, but maybe they're someone who freely gives the gift of time. Maybe they're that friend you can always count on to watch your pets while you're away, or who consistently checks in about a sick family member. Maybe they're the friend you know you can go to for good advice or they're the one who gives the best hugs. By learning to see the many ways our friends show up for us every day, you may find that you've been showered with gifts all along!

As for the gift-adverse, it's all about letting go for you, too. In order to do so, you may need to spend some time investigating why gifting gives you so much anxiety, and how to let go of that anxiety every once in a while to make sure your gift-giving friends feel loved and appreciated. Even if you're not a gift-giver yourself, you can still appreciate the time and care a friend put into picking out a special gift for you, and thank them accordingly. You also may benefit from expanding your definition of what counts as a gift. Maybe some of the gift anxiety that you're experiencing stems from an idea that gifts need to be expensive, ostentatious, or deeply meaningful to be of value. This couldn't be further from the truth! For people who truly value gift-giving as a love language, the point isn't the material value of what's being exchanged. The point is to feel seen and cared for. It makes them feel loved to know that they were on your mind during the holidays, on their birthday, or while you were perusing the street markets on your trip to Thailand. Once you expand your idea of a gift to include anything that lets a dear friend know they're on your mind, you may find that you feel significantly less pressure to get things "right" or find the "perfect" present.

In the modern era, gifts can also be virtual. Things like sending your friend an article they might be interested in or a video you think might make them laugh, is another way to communicate the very thing true gift lovers want to hear: I saw this and thought of you. These tiny exchanges can help you deepen your connection by filling your well of friendship with new jokes to laugh over and ideas to discuss. In many ways, they are the gifts that keep on giving as you draw from the well over and over again throughout the course of your friendship.

However, if you're really stuck on what to give your gift-loving friend, a heartfelt card always does wonders. You can even go back to your elementary-school days and make it out of macaroni! Who knows, you may be surprised to find it hanging on your friend's fridge the next time you go over for dinner.

FRIENDSHIP & ACTS OF SERVICE

Those of us who suffer from the modern disease of being "chronically online" may have noticed a disturbing idea pop up on social media over the last few years. I call it the cult of "You Don't Owe Anyone Anything." According to these posters, there's no reason ever to pick up a friend from the airport or help them move. In fact, even asking for these actions counts as "unpaid labor," and expecting it from anyone is a form of exploitation. Under this capitalistic worldview, the only reason ever to do anything for anyone else—even your friends—is if there is money involved. The values of altruism, community care, and mutual aid are thrown out the window.

When I see people, particularly young people, espousing this worldview it makes me profoundly sad. I'm not just sad over what it means to have a society where we don't see any reason to help one another (even the people we purport to like!), but it makes me sad for the person who thinks that way. Friendships are based on the idea of association without obligation. Old friends often represent the first relationships in our lives that arose completely by choice. You like them. They like you. So why not hang out at recess? One of the things that sets our friendships apart is the simple fact that these are people who have no reason to have your back and show up for you, but they do anyway. When we try to commodify every moment of connection and transform it into "emotional labor" that should be quantified and compensated, we lose the thing that makes friendship so special. No wonder young people these days are feeling so lonely.

What exactly do we owe our friends? Nothing—and that's kind of the point. We don't do acts of service for our friends because they pay us, or because they raised us, or because they file taxes with us. We do acts of service for our friends because we want to see them happy and cared for. We want them to know that we're with them through life's triumphs and challenges, and that by sticking together we can ensure that neither of us is ever alone. It's a beautiful, selfless ritual that brings us all a little closer to our best selves.

Alright, now that I've waxed poetic about the importance of acts of service in our friendships, we should probably talk about what acts of service in a friendship actually look like. Much like in our romantic relationships, acts of service are things we do to take something off a friend's plate. This can look like:

- Offering to babysit so your new-parent friends can have a date night.
- Ordering chicken noodle soup to a sick friend's house.
- Giving a friend a ride home, even if the destination is a little bit out of the way.
- Offering to walk a friend's dog when you know they're swamped with work.
- Stopping by to water a friend's houseplants while they're on vacation.
- Helping clear the table after they've had you over for dinner.

In short, acts of service can be anything that you offer freely and joyfully to a friend for no reason other than to show you care. These acts—small or large—can be absolutely transformational in a friend's life. Which is why I will now offer my last bit of advice: don't forget to offer acts of service to your friend who seems like they have it all under control. Sometimes they are the people in our lives who could use a helping hand the most. Stay attuned to which of your friends struggle with asking for help, and look for ways to show up without them having to say a word. Some people are so afraid of being rejected or judged when they ask for help that they pretend they don't need any. By simply noticing where they could use support and stepping in to help, you can not only provide them with relief with the problem at hand but also make them more likely to feel comfortable coming to you with problems in the future.

Helping our friends helps us to become better, healthier people. In fact, acts of service form another love language that's been linked to positive health outcomes such as reduced rates of depression, decreases in chronic pain, a strengthened immune system, lower blood pressure, and increased life expectancy. Not only do acts of service help our friends in times of need, but they also help us live longer, meaning we'll have even more time to spend with our friends! Lovely how that all works out, isn't it?

FRIENDSHIP & PHYSICAL TOUCH

We've already established all the ways that physical intimacy can be a powerful tool for human connection. In many of our love relationships, the bounds of physical touch can feel almost pre-determined. Romantic relationships are generally expected to include kissing, cuddling, and eventually, sex. Familial love means kisses from grandma, hugs from mom, and piggyback rides from dad. When it comes to friendship, however, the bounds of physical touch are less defined. Wanting to be touched is part of human nature, but how you and your friends want to use physical touch to express love may vary wildly based on a number of deeply personal factors such as:

- Past trauma.
- Sensory issues.
- Social anxiety.
- Cultural norms.
- Chronic pain or disability.
- Just good old-fashioned personal preference!

Figuring out the right amount of physical touch in your relationship with a friend means considering all of these factors and adjusting accordingly. While you may be a highly tactile person, who feels totally comfortable cuddling with a friend on the couch, someone else may find it stressful or invasive. Some friends may want nothing more than to be comforted with a hug, while others may find them awkward and prefer to have space. The only way you'll find out which of your friends is which is by asking, observing, and being open to what you find.

There is never anything wrong with having boundaries around physical intimacy, and nobody has a right to use physical touch to make anybody else uncomfortable. With that said, I want to issue the following challenge: look for more ways to incorporate physical intimacy with your friends.

If you're not someone who generally expresses themselves with physical touch, the idea of starting to do so in your platonic relationships may feel daunting, but it doesn't need to be! Physical touch among friends could mean anything from a high five to a hug, to a gentle hand on the shoulder when they're feeling upset. If both of you are touch-averse people, injecting more physical intimacy into your relationship could be more about proximity than actual touch: even something as simple as sitting next to each other on the couch and enjoying being in each other's space.

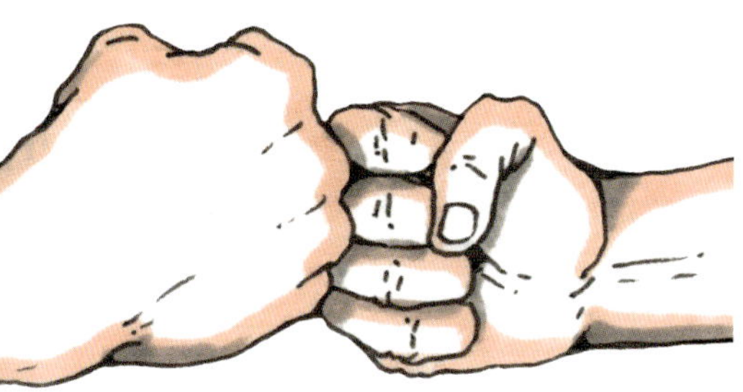

It may surprise you to know that physically intimate friendships used to be the norm, even among straight men. Nowadays, toxic masculinity and social stigma often prevent men from being physically expressive with their friends. Even to this day, it's not uncommon to hear a man jokingly yell, "No homo!" before even putting his arm around a friend. It's hard not to imagine that this lack of physical intimacy could be related to the rising levels of loneliness among cis, straight men. It's a sad symptom of patriarchy that was not the norm even fifty years ago. You don't have to turn the clock back far to find accounts of male friends holding hands, hugging each other, and even sharing a bed. Photos from as far back as the 1860s show male friends with their arms around each other, resting heads on each other's shoulders, or even sitting on each other's laps. While some of these men may have also been engaged in a romantic relationship, the sheer number of these photos speaks to a simpler truth: friends used to touch each other.

Unfortunately, our so-called "modern" sensibilities have taken us all—but particularly men—backward in terms of platonic touch. Starting in the mid-twentieth century, increasing social anxieties around homosexuality led to physical touch between friends becoming sexualized, especially if those friends were men. It's a sad loss. When all physical touch is perceived as romantic, it means an entire love language has been taken off the menu in our friendships. Chances are, you picked up this book because you want to try being more expansive with your expressions of love, not less. That's why I'm challenging you to find ways to bring physical touch into your friendships. As always, consent is key, but allowing for small moments of physical touch between friends could help us combat loneliness, and feel more connected to each other overall.

FRIENDSHIP & RESPECTING BOUNDARIES

Let's get this out of the way right up top: lack of boundaries is a huge friendship killer. It may feel good to engage in a boundaryless relationship with a friend at first. Friendships, just like romantic relationships, are susceptible to the "honeymoon phase." During this phase, the excitement around your new friendship may make it exciting to transgress any personal boundaries you have around communication, touch, and personal time. As you settle into the friendship, however, reestablishing these boundaries in a way that makes both friends feel safe and comfortable will be key to making the friendship work long-term.

Some boundaries you may need to set with a friend are:

- **I can't always respond to texts right away.**
- **I need you to let me know when you're coming over.**
- **I feel disrespected when you don't show up on time.**
- **[Insert sensitive subject] is actually a sensitive subject for me. I'd prefer if we talk about something else.**

Setting boundaries with a friend—or having a friend set boundaries with you—can be tough. It may feel like a rejection, or like you've done something wrong. In reality, a friend who sets boundaries is a friend who is putting in the effort to make the friendship work. Remember, a boundary is a vulnerable thing, often a product of our most deep-seated fears and most difficult experiences. Boundaries are often rooted in core memories or even traumas, and sharing them with another person is akin to trusting them with a secret. Friends who are able to see that vulnerability and respect our boundaries, despite their own emotions, are friends who are committed to making the relationship work. Friends who continue to trounce all over your boundaries because they feel differently or don't agree with them, are communicating a clear message: this relationship only works when it is on my terms.

Boundaries are a reflection of respect. Someone who refuses to abide by clearly stated boundaries is someone who does not respect you, your past, or your comfort. It can be incredibly painful to realize that someone who you consider a friend is incapable of showing you respect in the way you deserve. The truth is, their inability to respect your boundaries has little to do with you. Maybe they are used to a boundaryless homelife and have come to associate a lack of boundaries with love. Maybe they resent your ability to set boundaries in your life because they've never felt empowered to set boundaries in their own. Maybe they're just kind of a jerk. Whatever the reason, it's not your problem to solve. All you can do is set your boundaries, respect the boundaries that are set by others, recognize the friends who respect the boundaries you put in place, and leave behind the ones that don't.

FRIENDSHIP & EMOTIONAL SECURITY

Emotional security is the backbone of any strong friendship. Without it, why on earth would you want to stay friends? Emotional security is the reason our friends are often the first people we go to with problems in our other relationships. While you may fear how an anxious parent will react to the news that you've decided to quit your job, break up with your long-term partner, or dye your hair blue, your friends should always be a safe place to land.

Recently, I stumbled upon a Reddit page, called r/lostafriend, for people who have gone through friendship breakups. In one thread, commenters who had initiated a breakup of their own were asked to share why they ended things with their friend. Overwhelmingly, commenters cited one issue: a lack of emotional security. From friends with anger issues to

> EMOTIONAL SECURITY IS THE REASON OUR FRIENDS ARE OFTEN THE FIRST PEOPLE WE GO TO WITH PROBLEMS IN OUR OTHER RELATIONSHIPS.

friends who can't keep a secret, to friends with a nasty habit of dating your exes, a lack of emotional safety was turning out to be a veritable friendship serial killer. Many of the commenters even admitted to ghosting their ex-friend–disappearing with little to no communication as to why. While this can seem like a cruel way to end things with a friend, when a lack of emotional security is at play, it may be the only way a person feels safe extricating themselves from the friendship. A sense of emotional safety is what enables us to have difficult conversations with friends, which is often the first step to repairing a friendship that's been broken. If a person can't trust that they can do that without their friend lashing out in anger or becoming emotionally volatile, they may opt not to have the conversation at all. Instead, the emotionally volatile friend will find out they've been dumped after their texts go unanswered or they realize they've been blocked on social media.

So, how do we avoid ending up as fodder for r/lostafriend? While no friendship is ever guaranteed to last forever, providing emotional security can help our friendships weather hard times or end amicably once they've run their course. Emotional security in a friendship means both friends feel comfortable sharing their thoughts and feelings without fear of judgment. In a friendship, emotional security can look like all sorts of things. For example:

- Knowing you can trust a friend to keep the things you tell them private (even when they'd make a really juicy story to share with others).
- Being able to tell someone when they've hurt your feelings or made you upset.
- Being able to share your joys and successes without fear of resentment.
- Knowing that your friend is there to build you up, not tear you down.
- Freedom from abusive language, yelling, or insults.

Take the classic case of the "bridezilla," a figure I see come up over and over again in advice columns and on social

media. The story is almost always the same. A once thriving friendship (or entire friend group!) falls apart due to someone who took the idea of a wedding being their "special day" a little too far. There are the brides who get angry when friends don't attend multiple expensive events, demand members of the wedding party dye their hair, or even tell them to change their body to fit into a particular dress. Friends begin to fear meltdowns over the slightest pushback against the bridezilla's plans and learn to tolerate abusive behavior, knowing it will all be explained away as the stress of wedding planning. Because this is all leading up to the bride's "big day," no one feels emotionally secure enough in their friendship to be honest about how her behavior around the wedding is making them feel. Instead, the put-upon wedding party keeps their feelings to themselves (or the group chat they've created, just to vent) and resentment continues to build. Once it is time for her to actually walk down the aisle, the bride may have no idea that she's doing so surrounded by people who simply can't wait for the whole thing to be over. When she heads off on her honeymoon, she has no idea that she's leaving behind a friendship on life support.

Ultimately, friendships should be fun, enjoyable partnerships that enrich both sides equally. When one person's emotional dysregulation leads to a sense of emotional insecurity, the friendship becomes all about serving the emotionally volatile person. Now, one friend is constantly walking on eggshells to avoid upsetting the other, leading to secrets, resentment, and eventually, estrangement. In short: the friendship is no longer fun, meaning it is no longer a friendship at all.

> WE WANT TO BUILD FRIENDSHIPS WITH PEOPLE WHO CHALLENGE US AND, WHEN NECESSARY, CALL US OUT ON OUR CRAP.

FRIENDSHIP & HEALTHY DEBATE

Your friends aren't always going to agree with you. In fact, if they do, they're usually referred to as "yes men," not friends. We want to build friendships with people who challenge us and, when necessary, call us out on our crap. Enter: healthy debate.

Some friendships absolutely thrive on debate. These are the friends who love nothing more than to go out to a movie and argue about it afterward, go toe-to-toe at book club about why their favorite book is superior, or debate whether or not a certain musician is any

good. These are the friends who feel most connected when they're matching wits with another person and see their regular sparring matches as the ultimate sign of respect. Other friends may rarely find themselves on opposite sides of an argument. Regardless of whether debate is a regular part of your friendship or a rare occurrence, being able to disagree respectfully is going to make sure you are able to deal with conflict when it may arise.

Healthy debate in a friendship should follow the same principles as healthy debate in a romantic relationship. Debates between friends should be:

- **Respectful:** never resort to insults, threats, or cruel words.
- **Intellectually curious:** always seek to understand your friend's argument before you start to dismantle it.
- **Open:** the best debates are ones in which both people are open to changing their minds or seeing things in a new way.

In an era of increasing political polarization and misinformation, there may be times when we have to challenge our friends on beliefs that we find to be genuinely harmful. No one is under any obligation to stay friends with someone who espouses hateful views, and we all have to decide for ourselves where we draw the line when it comes to political differences with our friends. Sometimes, by engaging in healthy debate, we can help our friend open their mind to a new idea or way of seeing the world—and by listening with respect and openness ourselves, maybe we'll find places where our own minds need changing.

One of the most beautiful parts of a friendship is how our friends can change us and help us grow into better people. Engaging in healthy debate is part of that process. Even inconsequential debates over things such as which Spice Girl was the best dancer (Mel B, obviously) or what is the superior ice-cream flavor (mint chocolate chip) can teach us to be better listeners and open communicators. That way, when the time comes to have more serious debates with our friends, we'll have all the tools we need to engage them in a healthy, loving way.

> ONE OF THE MOST BEAUTIFUL PARTS OF A FRIENDSHIP IS HOW OUR FRIENDS CAN CHANGE US AND HELP US GROW INTO BETTER PEOPLE.

FRIENDSHIP & SHARED GOALS & EXPERIENCES

We've already talked about what can happen in a friendship when life stages are mismatched, but what about the special magic that can happen when goals and experiences are shared? There's a reason why formative experiences such as high school, college, first apartments, and jobs can all produce lifelong friendships. When you experience these life phases together, the shared memories from that time in your life strengthen your bond. Sure, I can tell the friends I make now all about the dirty house my boyfriend lived in at college, but only my friends who were there will be able to picture the mile-high pile of dirty dishes in the sink, or the unspeakable condition of the bathroom.

While new life phases may strain some friendships, they will strengthen others. Friends who become new parents at the same time can bond over the ups and downs of pregnancy, or how lack of sleep is taking its toll. Friends who grow apart for a time may reconnect over the shared experience of losing a parent and use each other for support. We can also create new life experiences with friends by taking trips

or seeing your favorite artist in concert: shared experiences are memories, and memories are bonds. By continuing to share new experiences with our friends when we can, we're building new bonds that will help us get through the times when communication is limited or when life phases aren't aligned.

Shared goals can also be incredible ways to deepen a friendship. I know friends who have trained for marathons together, started book clubs together, and even made a pact to learn a new language together. Not only did the companionship help them stick to their goals, but it helped them to get to know each other by taking on a challenge together. Some may say, "never mix business with friendship," but many successful business owners started as friends first. Companies such as Airbnb, Microsoft, and even Ben & Jerry's were all companies founded by people who were friends first. Clearly, shared goals were a big part of their menu of love—also mint chocolate chip.

QUIZ

FRIENDSHIP LOVE LANGUAGES

Still not sure exactly how you want to express love in your friendships? Well, you're in luck because we've developed another quiz to help you figure it out! Read each question and tally up your responses. At the end, you'll have your very own ranking to show which of our nine love languages you gravitate toward most, and which you may need to pay a little more attention to in order to become fluent. You may never identify strongly with your lowest-ranked love language, but learning to understand it will help you to be a better friend to those who do. Come back to this quiz any time you think your ranking may have changed.

Read each of the following statements and circle the answer that best describes you, then turn to page 156 to discover your Friendship Love Languages preferences.

E My best friends are the people I talk to every day.

B My best friends are the people I can talk to about anything.

I My best friends are the people who show up for me without me even having to ask.

D My best friends are the people I've known the longest.

A Disrespect is my biggest friendship red flag.

C Over-sensitivity is my biggest friendship red flag.

F Lack of intimacy is my biggest friendship red flag.

H Thoughtlessness is my biggest friendship red flag.

C I love a friend who will tell me when I'm wrong.

H I love a friend who never comes over empty-handed.

F I love a friend who gives good hugs.

E I love a friend who always picks up when I call.

A It makes me feel seen when a friend notices my triggers.

D It makes me feel seen when a friend notices my accomplishments.

G It makes me feel seen when a friend knows just what to say.

I It makes me feel seen when a friend offers to help.

H My BFF's best quality is that they are a good listener.

B My BFF's best quality is that they always make me feel safe.

A My BFF's best quality is that they accept me for who I am.

I My BFF's best quality is that they are selfless.

C I would end a friendship over the other person's inability to argue.

E I would end a friendship over too many canceled plans.

F I would end a friendship over a lack of physical closeness.

G I would end a friendship if they never had anything nice to say.

D My most fulfilling friendships are active—we're always trying new things!

B My most fulfilling friendships are emotional—we wear our hearts on our sleeves!

C My most fulfilling friendships keep me on my toes—we love to playfully tease!

A My most fulfilling friendships are easy—we just understand each other!

G Communication is fundamental to a healthy friendship.

F Intimacy is fundamental to a healthy friendship.

H Thoughtfulness is fundamental to a healthy friendship.

I Selflessness is fundamental to a healthy friendship.

A I want a friend who understands my history.

B I want a friend who understands my heart.

C I want a friend who challenges me intellectually.

D I want a friend who loves to try new things with me.

B I want friends who make me feel safe.

D I want friends who share my hopes and dreams.

G I want friends who tell me that they care.

E I want friends who make time for me in their life.

I A friend who helps me move is the best.

H A friend who brings me a souvenir when they travel is the best.

E A friend who makes time to just hang out is the best.

F A friend who lets me cry on their shoulder is the best.

G A friend who says "I love you" is the best.

LOVE LANGUAGES & FAMILY

Familial love is oftentimes the first form of love we're introduced to, mere moments after we're born. We all know what familial love is supposed to be–kind, comfortable, and unconditional. In reality, we also know that familial relationships can be complicated. Sometimes, our family members are the people we struggle the most to express our love to, even when the love is there. The fact that two people are related does not necessarily mean that they're going to express love in the same way. A family of four may have four completely different ways of communicating love and care. When it comes to kids, they may end up preferring the exact love language that their parent struggles most to speak. Mismatched love languages between parents, siblings, grandparents, and cousins can all lead to pain and confusion in familial relationships, even when all parties genuinely love and care for each other. By learning to speak all of the love languages, we can start to understand our family members better and have better communication with them.

One of the most beautiful things familial love offers us is the chance to forge multigenerational relationships. Elders can impart wisdom to the young, and the young are able to challenge their elders and prevent them from getting too stuck in outdated beliefs. In order to make this intergenerational relationship work, we have to be curious. Growing up in different generations may mean love is expressed in different ways. Aunts and uncles may have to learn to value a text the same way they value a phone

call, and younger siblings may have to learn to endure the occasional in-person visit to grandma, even though she doesn't have wifi.

There are, of course, familial relationships that are unable to be repaired. For those who have found their family's love was conditional upon their ability to endure abuse or hide an integral part of themselves, no amount of work with the love languages is going to fix the problem. In the queer community, which faces much higher levels of estrangement from biological family members, the idea of a "chosen family" has taken hold. A chosen family is a group of people who are not necessarily related but have agreed to show up for each other in the way their biological families have failed to do. They affirm each other's gender identities and sexuality, show up for holidays, and generally support each other in the ways that society says a mother, father, brother, or sister should. In essence, they've agreed to learn to speak each other's love languages together and forge a different type of familial bond based on mutual respect.

FAMILY & WORDS OF AFFIRMATION

Family members—especially siblings—often have a unique ability to push each other's buttons. Somehow, they always know what to say to get your blood pressure soaring. What we sometimes fail to realize is that this superpower can also be used for good. Just the same way that you know what to say to annoy your dad at dinner, you also know what to say to build him up. Think about any member of your family that you're relatively close with. Chances are, you already have some ideas about their hopes, insecurities, and values. You know how important it is to your Aunt Susan that you notice her new hairstyle, or how hard your sibling worked to save up for their first car. You know how much care your brother puts into maintaining his car, or how much pride your mom takes in her garden. When it comes to expressing love through words of affirmation with a family member, you probably already know the right words to use. The challenge is remembering to say them.

Sometimes, you may be dealing with a family member who is stingy with their words of affirmation. Maybe one or both of your parents struggled with expressing their love through encouraging words, and now that's the love language you crave most. While you'll probably never be able to change a person who doesn't naturally express their love with words, you can lead by example. If you want to change your family's relationship around words of affirmation, try being generous with words of affirmation yourself. That doesn't mean showering them with empty compliments in hopes of receiving one in return—compliments must be genuinely and generously given to be meaningful. However, by simply modeling what a relationship with more kindness and encouragement looks like, you may see the way your family uses words of affirmation start to change.

FAMILY & QUALITY TIME

Every culture in the world has rituals around spending quality time with family. Holidays, birthdays, weddings, and funerals are all events designed around ensuring that families get together and stay connected. Getting together as a family builds strong, multigenerational ties with proven benefits such as decreased loneliness and depression, and even better performance in

school. However, it would be a lie to say that maintaining these relationships is always easy. As we grow older, we may find ourselves living further and further away from mom and dad, as we move for school and work. If you start to have a family of your own, the difficulties, expense, and stress of traveling with children may further complicate efforts to get together for family events. If quality time is something your family truly values, it may be that everyone has to make adjustments to ensure that the family can still get together in a stress-free way.

What does this look like? For one, family members should be mindful of who is always hosting, and who is always traveling. Oftentimes, younger members of the family are expected to travel back to their hometowns for the holidays, even though they are also often the family members with less disposable income and flexibility at work. What would it look like for your family if you took the holiday celebrations elsewhere every once in a while? Sure, it may *feel* unthinkable to open Christmas presents anywhere but in front of the tree at grandma's house, but the beautiful thing about quality time is that actually it can happen anywhere.

Holidays and milestone celebrations are a great way to ensure we all spend quality time with family, but you also can't expect to maintain a relationship while only seeing each other a few times a year. Luckily, there's a little thing called the telephone that's been around for about 150 years. Use it. Call your mother. Call your grandmother. Call your younger sibling even though you know they're not going to pick up, because maybe if you do it enough times they eventually will. Agree to meet up with your cousin, if they're passing through your city, even if you're not as close as you were as kids. Developing and maintaining relationships with family members takes work. It means older generations reaching out to younger generations to let them know they have support. It means younger generations stepping up to help older generations as they need support of their own. While you may not always be able to be together in person, something as simple as a family group chat can do wonders for making sure everybody stays connected and keeps in touch—even if you do have to leave it on mute most of the time. We all know Aunt Linda can get a bit overzealous with the early morning messages . . .

FAMILY & RECEIVING GIFTS

Often, family gift-giving can be a minefield. From the uncle who likes to use gifts as an opportunity to show off his wealth or the cousin who perpetually "forgets" his contribution to the secret Santa, what should be a selfless expression of care between loved ones can be anything but. You can't control how your family members act around gifts. All you can do is give your own gifts from a genuine place and receive them with genuine gratitude. Being a good gift-giver is rooted in being a good listener. Even if you have a mom who perpetually insists she "doesn't want anything" for birthdays and holidays, or a dad who seems impossible to shop for, chances are, you could probably come up with *something* to make them smile.

What makes a good gift? It's not the price tag or the difficulty it took to get. A good gift is something that makes the receiver feel seen. Here's a story from my own life: my mother's youngest brother, who is autistic, loves music. One year, on my way down to visit my family for Christmas, I realized that I'd forgotten to get my uncle a gift. Panicked, I grabbed something that to most people would represent the worst, most impersonal gift imaginable: a Spotify gift card. But I had a feeling, knowing my uncle, that it just might work out. When I presented it to him on Christmas Day, I was slightly embarrassed. Then, as I helped him download the Spotify app and showed him how to use it to listen to whatever music he wanted on demand (and ad-free, thanks to my gift card), his eyes lit up. Suddenly, he had access to all his favorite songs at the touch of a button—something he didn't even realize was possible. He spent the rest of the night searching the Spotify archives, gleefully playing new songs for us every time he realized one of his favorites was available. I don't tell you this story to pat myself on the back for my gift-giving skills (though I did kind of knock it out of the park with this one) but rather to show how something as simple as a gift card you panic buy from the nearest grocery store can end up being a great gift if it's chosen with the receiver in mind.

> **ALL YOU CAN DO IS GIVE YOUR OWN GIFTS FROM A GENUINE PLACE AND RECEIVE THEM WITH GENUINE GRATITUDE.**

This doesn't mean that you need to stress yourself out trying to find something completely unique for every individual. It just means paying attention to someone's likes, dislikes, life phases, and living situation, and making a genuine effort to give a gift that reflects those things. If you know someone will be traveling via airplane to get back home, don't gift them something that's going to take up half their suitcase. In fact, they'd probably be more than happy to receive a gift card that they can easily tuck into their carry-on and use on a gift of their choosing later. Sure, a gift card may *usually* seem a bit impersonal, but in this instance, it actually reflects the exact things every gift should be trying to communicate: consideration and care. And to be honest . . . who doesn't love a good gift card? It's free money!

FAMILY & ACTS OF SERVICE

Here's a scene that may be familiar within a lot of families: mom cooks dinner. Mom serves dinner. Mom cleans up dinner. Mom finally eats her own dinner cold over the sink after everyone else is done. The divide of domestic chores in heterosexual marriages has become more equitable in recent years, but research shows that women are still saddled with the majority of household tasks. So, when it comes to acts of service in your family, the moms should be the first place you look to lend a helping hand. If you notice that your own family expects more from its women than its men when it comes to cooking, cleaning, and hosting duties, be the one to speak up and make a change. Offer to lend a helping hand yourself and see if you can enlist some of the men of the family to join you in cleaning up the table or serving drinks. Sure, you may get some grumbles and dirty looks from the older generation, but by encouraging family members to notice when someone is doing the lion's share of the work, you can encourage everyone to engage in more acts of service across the board.

When expressing love to a family member through acts of service, make sure that the acts of service you're offering are actually helpful and desired. As much as it may seem as if grandma wants help in the kitchen, she may actually find the presence of an extra person–who she will inevitably have to coach through the exact preparations for her famous casserole–to be more stressful than helpful. You may find older family

members resistant to accepting acts of service as a point of pride, not wanting to admit that a task they once easily accomplished is getting harder. Be gentle here. If the point of an act of service is to make someone feel loved and cared for, forcing help on someone who isn't ready to accept it will not achieve that goal. Make the offer, and even if it is rejected in the moment, you may find that your family member comes back around to wanting your help, once they've had time to sit with the idea (or when their gutters finally reach the point of no return.)

Acts of service in a family can look like all sorts of things. It can look like everyone in the family taking turns holding the baby so parents can get a break, or setting aside time when you come home to help mow the lawn now that your parents are getting on in years. It can look like listening and giving life advice to a younger family member or helping an older family member declutter their home. In many ways, acts of service are the backbone of familial love. In a loving family, members know that they can count on one another to lend a helping hand. When acts of service are prized in a family, everyone works together for the greater good of the whole.

If that's not what family is for, then what is?

FAMILY & PHYSICAL TOUCH

"Give grandma a kiss!"
"Give your uncle a hug!"
"Let me squeeze those cheeks!"

The expectation that physical touch will be welcomed among family members is often engrained in us from a young age. Nowadays, parents are starting to shift this paradigm by focusing on their children's physical autonomy at a young age, allowing them to refuse unwanted hugs and kisses to teach them about the importance of consent. For those family members whose bids for physical touch were rejected, this can be painful, but the lesson that hurt feelings should never take precedence over consent is an important one.

That said, we shouldn't fear consensual physical touch and intimacy between family members. In fact, the benefits of physical touch between members of the same family start from the moment you're born. Skin-to-skin contact between mothers and their newborn babies has proven health benefits for both such as:

> THE BENEFITS OF PHYSICAL TOUCH BETWEEN MEMBERS OF THE SAME FAMILY START FROM THE MOMENT YOU'RE BORN.

- Regulation of the baby's vital signs such as heart rate, blood sugar, temperature, and oxygen levels.
- Release of the "love" hormone oxytocin for both mom and baby, plus others that help support breastfeeding.
- Helping build the baby's immunity to infections.
- Providing pain relief for both mother and baby after birth.
- Less stress and crying for the baby.
- Helping to regulate postpartum bleeding, blood pressure, and stress hormones for the birthing parent.
- Promoting bonding between the parents and child.

By contrast, babies deprived of physical touch in infancy can face a host of developmental issues, including behavioral problems and hormonal dysregulation. These children can grow up to experience greater rates of stress and depression, and even have been found to be more susceptible to eating disorders and "overly compliant or subdued behaviors." Clearly, safe and loving touch is an important part of a child's development, so it is the responsibility of older family members to help show younger ones exactly what that means.

We've talked about how to navigate physical touch between adult family members and children, but physical

intimacy between two adult family members can present its own benefits and challenges. Physical intimacy in a family is incredibly personal and is often dictated by things such as history and cultural norms. Once you reach adulthood, you probably already know which family members are going to greet you with a big bear hug as soon as you reach the door, and which ones would be uncomfortable going beyond a nod or a handshake. Part of navigating the love language of physical touch within a family isn't just about being mindful of your own boundaries but also keeping an eye out for the boundaries of others so that they can feel safe and comfortable around you as well.

And just when you feel as if you've finally gotten your own family figured out . . . here come the in-laws. As your family expands to include new members, with their own history and cultural norms, you may have to learn a whole new playbook for how physical touch is used. In some families, a kiss on the cheek is an expected greeting. In others, doing so might be seen as overly familiar or strange. Some families identify as "huggers," while other families are totally fine keeping their distance. Joining a new family often involves some awkward moments, which is why it's always good to check in with your partner about their family's norms and preferences so that you know what you're getting into (and so they can run interference when you and your new nana-in-law's touch preferences aren't aligned).

FAMILY & RESPECTING BOUNDARIES

For many people, family and boundaries simply do not go together. The closeness of familial relationships, the intimacy that exists between household members, and cultural expectations around respect for elders can all get in the way of making someone feel comfortable setting boundaries within a family. If you're the first family member to try and break the toxic cycle of boundaryless relationships, you probably already know that you've got your work cut out for you. Setting boundaries with family members who don't have experience with receiving them can be difficult. Some common boundaries that family members may find themselves having to establish with one another are:

- "I will not be lending you any more money."
- "I won't discuss my relationship, if you can't be respectful."
- "How we parent [adorable grandbaby] isn't up for debate."
- "I hate that nickname and I'm not responding to it."

The list goes on and on—especially once grandkids get into the mix and one generation's parenting style goes head-to-head with another. It's easy to avoid conversations like this because, let's be honest, they're incredibly stressful! Yet, they're also opportunities for family members to ask for and receive love from one another.

A common boundary that I've seen my friends use with their parents—especially daughters with their moms—is around how they talk about weight, food, and bodies in general. Enter the "almond mom," a much talked-about character on social media, who represents a common experience among many women. The almond mom is obsessed with food. She's always counting calories and offering "a handful of almonds" as a snack, insisting that it's just as satisfying as a bag of chips or a bar of chocolate. "A moment on the lips, a lifetime on the hips!" is the motto she lives by, and she wants the other women in her life, particularly her daughters and granddaughters, to live by the same code. The almond mom watches her weight—and her daughter's weight—like a hawk, and just can't help but comment on every perceived change on the scale, always with a tone of trying to "help."

In many cases, the almond mom genuinely means well. She grew up in a time when a woman's worth was directly correlated to her thinness, and she has genuine fears for her

daughter's future if she fails to meet these standards. While we're hardly in an age beyond fatphobia or body stigma for women, it's time for the almond mom and her mentality to go—and millennial and Gen-Z women are the ones showing her the door. I can't tell you how many times I've heard about friends having a hard talk with their mothers about cutting out conversations around weight, food, and bodies. Some take it better than others. For some people, establishing a boundary is always going to be received as a personal attack, and their inability to set their ego aside and honor their loved one's request can lead to missed holidays, frayed connections, and even painful periods of estrangement. For some almond moms, the temptation to comment on "baby weight" or clock extra helpings of dessert is more important than respecting their child's boundary, and despite claims that they're doing it all out of love, actually they've communicated the opposite: "I love you . . . but I'd love you more if you were thin."

On the flip side, former almond moms who rose to the challenge to change how they spoke about food at their child's request—even if they didn't fully understand or agree—strengthened their relationships with this show of love. I think back to a friend of mine who had to set this very boundary with her mother, and the clear feeling of love and happiness in her eyes as she explained over dinner one night that on her last trip home she had seen her mother actively making an effort to curb food-related commentary (and during Thanksgiving, no less!). The issues of body negativity and food policing had been a decades-long problem between this friend and her mother, but with the very act of hearing and accepting her daughter's thoughtfully established boundary, the process of healing could begin.

This same experience is mirrored in the lives of queer folks, who often have to put up strong boundaries with family members who are struggling to accept their identity. Those family members who can respect those boundaries as they work through their own prejudices, often come out on the other side as their queer family member's fiercest advocates. One of my favorite advice columnists and podcasters, Dan Savage, often speaks about witnessing this transformation with his own deeply Catholic mother. Those parents who are unable to prioritize their children's boundaries over their bigotry, are the ones who often find themselves shut out of their queer child's life in favor of a chosen family that respects them for who they are.

That's why respecting healthy boundaries is such a powerful love language. It has the ability to show both sides of the love coin, displaying either a relationship's strength or its need for a quick dissolution.

FAMILY & EMOTIONAL STABILITY

Anxiety can be inherited. So can depression. The way we express our emotions is heavily impacted by how we saw them being expressed by the adults in our lives when we were growing up. While family *should* be the place where we all feel safest to go with our highest highs and lowest lows, unfortunately that is not always the case. We all know people (or perhaps we *are* the people) who don't feel like they can go to their parents with problems for fear of their outsized reaction. When a parent-child relationship lacks emotional security, it can lead to simmering resentments and, eventually, outright hostility. Parents should be their child's safe harbor–a place they always know that they can return to for comfort and understanding. When a parent or guardian fails to provide that for their child, they can end up with a child who keeps secrets or hides their true emotions for fear of how the adults in their life will act. This can lead to all sorts of problems, from teenagers who drink and drive because they're more afraid of getting in trouble at home than they are of the dire consequences of getting behind the wheel while intoxicated, to young adults who feel the need to hide their romantic partners from their family for fear they'll be harshly judged or treated poorly. Nothing kills a familial relationship like a lack of emotional security, which is why parents should make providing an emotionally secure environment one of their top priorities.

Sometimes, an entire family is held hostage by the emotional volatility of one of its members. These are the aunts who are constantly on the lookout for perceived slights, the uncles who can't stop themselves from making polarizing political comments at dinner, and the cousins

who think every family gathering should revolve around them and their drama. It's amazing how one person's volatility can affect the emotional security of the whole, but it happens all the time. When it happens in a family, it can be even harder to draw the necessary boundaries to bring things back into equilibrium, especially when the emotionally volatile person is surrounded by enablers. Oftentimes, everyone agrees that a family member's behavior is out of line, but it has been tolerated for so long everyone just accepts it as normal.

It's not. A truly loving family environment should be a safe, non-judgmental space for all its members. No one should spend the lead up to what is supposed to be a joyful family gathering, worried about how one person is going to behave or strategizing what to do when they inevitably get out of line. Establishing emotional security in these instances will mean having some hard conversations, putting in place firm boundaries, and, if necessary, creating an entirely separate space for family members who want to be emotionally secure. If you do this, don't be surprised if you're made out to be the bad guy or are accused of tearing the family apart. All you can do is create a safe space for yourself and those who want to join you, secure in the knowledge that actually you're doing the best thing possible to keep the family together.

FAMILY & HEALTHY DEBATE

You may be thinking, "Healthy debate? In *my* family?!? Not a chance!" As we already said, nobody knows how to get under our skin quite like a family member. Siblings are often our first (and fiercest) sparring partners in debates that can end up lasting for years, even decades. In the USA, jokes abound about the prevalence of heated political arguments around the Thanksgiving dinner table, and depictions of screaming matches between teenagers and their parents are all over TV, movies, and literature.

But what if it doesn't have to be this way? What if we can actually engage our family members in healthy debates, based on a foundation of respect, without it ending in ruined holidays, tears, or estrangement? I believe that this can happen, but only if we all agree to stick to some ground rules. For example:

- Listen openly.
- No personal attacks.
- No raised voices.
- No talking over each other or interrupting.

Easier said than done, I know, especially when your debate partner isn't as committed to the rules of healthy debate as you are. Which brings us to our next point: if a family member can't debate in a healthy, respectful way . . . then don't debate them.

You are always well within your rights to end a conversation if you're being disrespected or simply bombarded by another person, who has no intention of listening to what you have to say. Just as we said in our section introducing healthy debate as a love language, this does not mean that you should tolerate debates where your human rights or the validity of your identity is being questioned. Those debates are not coming from a place of love, and you do not need to engage with them.

The one exception to this rule . . . teenagers. If you're the parent of a teenager, or you've got a teenage

> SIBLINGS ARE OFTEN OUR FIRST (AND FIERCEST) SPARRING PARTNERS IN DEBATES THAT CAN END UP LASTING FOR YEARS, EVEN DECADES.

shared experiences to draw upon together. When family members live separately due to things such as divorce or other factors, it can create new challenges for expressing love through shared experiences. In these instances, family members will have to take it upon themselves to make sure they're still creating memories together, even when they're apart. Even in a joint-custody situation, both parents can still express love through shared experiences with their child, even if their co-parent isn't present. In fact, it may be more important than ever to focus on creating shared experiences during this time so that the child can still feel a sense of normalcy. If they're used to conversing in the shared experiences love language and suddenly it disappears, this can make a confusing, painful time even more confusing and painful. Luckily, shared experiences can be as simple as seeing a movie together, or a regular Sunday night dinner at dad's favorite pizza place.

When it comes to shared goals, this can play out differently for different families. Oftentimes, families have one clear, overarching goal: to be a happy, healthy, and successful family unit. However, what this looks like for one person may look different for another, and conflict can arise when one family member's ideas about success differs wildly from another's. Sure, grandpa may have a goal of having

family member in your life, you may need to model how healthy debate as a love language works before they're able to start using it themselves. This may mean you, as the adult, will have to tolerate some unhealthy debating strategies from your opponent while you remain healthy yourself. It may not be fun to deal with a young person who is behaving this way, but you're doing the world a service by helping someone grow into a healthier, more loving debater as an adult. Who knows? Maybe their future partner will send you a thank-you gift! (If that's one of their love languages, of course.)

FAMILY & SHARED GOALS AND EXPERIENCES

Within a family, shared experiences typically come pretty easily. Between family trips, holiday celebrations, that time the dog ate an entire chocolate cake and had to have his stomach pumped, and the general ins and outs of everyday life, you and your family members will likely have a lot of

as many grandbabies as possible, but his children may have different plans. Nobody likes to be pressured to have kids, especially if they've already been clear that they don't want any. Sometimes, the family "goal" of creating as many new members as possible can get in the way of seeing all the other things someone has achieved. This can lead single or child-free family members to grow resentful as every new baby is greeted with family-wide fanfare, but the completion of their masters degree or their new promotion goes totally unnoticed.

Remember, family members should be each other's biggest cheerleaders. Even if someone's goals look different to yours, you can still share in their joy for having accomplished it. Be curious, take notice of what your family members are working toward, and let them know you're proud of them when they meet their milestones. Just because you would never be caught dead running a marathon doesn't mean you can't share in your cousin's joy by cheering her on from the sidelines when she does. People tend to remember who was there with them for the big moments of joy in their life, and will hopefully return the favor when you're the one in need of congratulations.

QUIZ

FAMILY LOVE LANGUAGES

Now it's time to figure out how love is expressed in your family. By taking some time to analyze the ways your family gives and receives love and comparing it to your own preferences, you can learn a lot about how you can all start speaking the same love language. In places where you find you and your family are mismatched, you can move forward with a greater understanding of how your family operates and what you can do to receive more love in the way that is most meaningful to you. Tally up your answers for each entry below and you'll have a good idea of how your family expresses love with one another. Don't be afraid to share the results in the family group chat, or even to share this quiz with other members of the family so they can complete it on their own!

Read each of the following statements and circle the answer that best describes you, then turn to page 156 to discover your Family Love Languages preferences.

A — My family prioritizes in-person get togethers.
B — My family prioritizes physical affection between one another.
E — My family prioritizes showing up when someone is in need.
I — My family prioritizes working alongside one another.

F — My family does its best to be respectful of my feelings.
G — My family does its best to create a safe, calm, and secure environment.
H — My family does its best to agree to disagree.
D — My family does its best to make sure everyone feels included.

H — My family isn't afraid to challenge each other intellectually.
D — My family is generous with one another.
B — My family is physically affectionate with each other.
A — My family is never too far away.

F — My family values following the rules.
I — My family values accomplishments.
C — My family values compliments.
G — My family values a peaceful environment.

D I love that my family is generous with gifts.

G I love that my family is non-judgmental.

F I love that my family respects each other's wishes.

E I love that my family is always there for each other.

H My family never misses a chance to argue—our family game nights are intense!

A My family never misses a chance to get together—every year there's a reunion!

E My family never misses a chance to lend a helping hand—lemme grab the toolbox and I'll be right over!

C My family never misses a chance to say "I love you"—it's just how we feel!

I Sometimes my family can be too goals-oriented.

B Sometimes my family can be too touchy-feely.

H Sometimes my family can be loud.

A Sometimes my family can be clingy.

F I always know my family will respect my requests.

G I always know my family will make me feel safe.

C I always know my family will have something nice to say.

I I always know my family will cheer me on.

G My family would never tolerate emotional abuse.

I My family would never tolerate pessimistic behavior.

H My family would never tolerate someone who can't hear they're wrong.

F My family would never tolerate disrespect.

E Nothing would cause more drama in my family than someone not showing up to help.

D Nothing would cause more drama in my family than someone messing up the gift exchange.

A Nothing would cause more drama in my family than someone flaking on an important family event.

B Nothing would cause more drama in my family than someone refusing a hug.

C Nothing would cause more drama in my family than someone getting caught talking badly behind someone else's back.

LOVE LANGUAGES AT WORK

Yes, we can express love to coworkers—even the ones we swear we'd be happy to never see again. These expressions of love won't be the same as with your friends, family, or romantic partners (and if you do find a romantic partner at work, how you express love to them is a question for HR), but they'll be expressions of love nonetheless.

The fact of the matter is, if you have a traditional job then you are likely to be spending an enormous amount of time with your coworkers. So, why not make an effort to create a loving relationship between yourself and the people you spend forty hours a week with? Not only will the love languages make your office a better environment for you, but they may also help to change the company culture for everyone else. If you're stuck in a toxic work environment, it's probably a tall order to say that one single person can change what is likely to be a company-wide issue, possibly stemming from its leadership. But, could you make the office a happier place for yourself? Your desk mate? Your team? Yes, absolutely . . . while also submitting your résumé to work somewhere else, because no one needs to work in a place that makes them unhappy.

Many people meet some of their best friends or even their romantic partners at work. "Work wife," "work husband," and "work bestie" are all terms we've come up with to quantify the special relationships we build with the people who help us get through the work day. It's really no surprise that we may end up developing deep, long-lasting relationships with a group of people who have all chosen to work in the same field as us. People I worked with at various jobs when I was younger have become genuine friends, long after we both moved onto different opportunities. Some former coworkers even stood beside me at my wedding!

In recent years, there has been much criticism of companies that insist they are a "family," in order to extract more (often unpaid and unrecognized) labor from their employees. The rightful pushback against this kind of language has led to many younger people entering the workforce wary of mixing the personal and professional, out of fear that it will be used to guilt trip them into taking on a higher workload later on. While it's totally understandable to want to create strong boundaries around your work and personal time (more on that later on . . .), it's still important to find ways to be your true self while you're at work. Sure, you may not share all the details of your personal life at every morning meeting, but turning yourself into a work-focused robot devoid of all human emotion for eight hours a day is no way to live, either. The line between being professional and keeping yourself open to genuine connection will be different for everyone. That's where our trusty love languages come in! When you're at work, the love languages can be employed in a thoughtful, professional way to help you stay connected to your humanity while on the job and also help you to make your workplace better to be in overall.

In short: love what you do, and, ideally, also the people you do it with.

> DON'T LET FEAR OF HOW YOU'LL COME ACROSS STOP YOU FROM GIVING PRAISE WHERE PRAISE IS DUE.

COWORKERS & WORDS OF AFFIRMATION

Telling the people you work with when they're doing a good job is one of the simplest ways that we can make the workplace a happier, more encouraging place for everyone. Just as our friends, family, and romantic partners may not realize the things that make them great, your favorite coworkers may not realize how much their hard work is seen and appreciated. I mean, do you always know how much your hard work is seen and appreciated? Sometimes in the workplace, we're all so focused on our own tasks that we forget to notice how much is being done just a few feet away. We all know how much it means to have our own work recognized, so why not go out of our way to give that feeling of accomplishment to others?

Try something like:

- "Thanks for getting this in before the deadline! You're always so reliable and I really appreciate it."
- "You're such a good writer—this hardly needs any edits!"
- "You ran the heck out of that meeting today."
- "I love the energy you bring to the office; it really helps the day go by faster."
- "Your email sign-offs always make me laugh!"
- "That proposal you wrote was so great it inspired me to write one of my own!"

You don't have to limit your praise to your coworkers. Even the boss can use some encouragement in their leadership style from time to time (which could, in turn, make them a better leader). A word of caution, however—don't lay it on too thick. A constant shower of praise may come off as false or make people uncomfortable, and repeatedly hyping up your boss may seem as if you're just trying to get ahead in the workplace. As with all words of affirmation, the encouragement you give should be genuine and free from expectation. People can tell when praise has an ulterior motive, or when someone's positivity is shallow.

Of course, don't let fear of how you'll come off stop you from giving praise where praise is due. The point isn't to make you second guess yourself, it's just to be cognizant of what is motivating your desire to give a compliment in the workplace, and to stick to comments that are rooted in authentic admiration.

Once you authentically admire your coworkers, you'll enjoy spending more time with them, which leads us perfectly into our next love language . . .

COWORKERS & QUALITY TIME

The work-from-home culture that built up after the COVID-19 pandemic has a lot of benefits. Employees who work from home, or who have a hybrid workplace, report a better work-life balance, less stress commuting, fewer distractions, increased productivity, increased job satisfaction, and even better health as individuals are able to work in the way that is best suited to their needs. There's a lot to love about working from home, but there is one thing that is lost when an office goes fully remote: quality time between coworkers.

These days, the concept of casual "water-cooler conversations" now seems like a relic of a bygone era. When I first got into the workforce, after-work drinks were common among my friends with office jobs as a way to bond with their coworkers (and vent about the boss as needed). Meanwhile, holiday parties, weekend bonding "boot camps," and even company-wide cruises were all common ways for an employer to try and create opportunities for quality time between employees. While this type of forced bonding might make the modern worker cringe, it did serve a valuable purpose.

It's understandable and valid that many people like to keep their work and social spheres totally separate and prefer to keep their working relationships strictly professional. Quality time with coworkers need not be overly personal or the alcohol-soaked bacchanals on the TV show *Mad Men*, where over-the-top holiday parties and "liquid lunches" gave way to all manner of inappropriate office behavior. (It may have made for great TV, but it's certainly not how we want to conduct ourselves in the workplace today. Sorry, Don.) That said, professional relationships can

still be human, empathetic, and even fun, if we leave a little room for something other than work.

Some examples of quality time you may not even realize you're spending with coworkers are:

- **The five minutes you spend chit-chatting before the start of your morning meeting.**
- **Grabbing lunch together at your favorite local spot.**
- **Attending office celebrations for holidays, birthdays, or major milestones.**
- **Carpooling or commuting together on the train.**

Quality time with coworkers is important because it helps you get to know them as people. It helps to build empathy and a shared language between everyone on the team. It's not about making best friends or creating the dreaded "our office is a family" culture that younger workers wholeheartedly reject. Rather, it's about finding new ways to get to know each other and to get a fuller picture of each of your coworkers as human beings. You may never like Jerry from IT, but spending a little time talking to him about something other than your laptop's security, settings might help you to understand a little more about what makes him tick (and make you less irritated when he scolds you for falling for a phishing scam, again).

COWORKERS & RECEIVING GIFTS

When it comes to traditional gifting, chances are your office has either hard-and-fast rules, or generally understood norms, around what is appropriate for gift exchanges between coworkers. There may be designated gift-giving opportunities centered around holidays, birthday celebrations, or the recognition of other milestones such as the birth of a child, weddings, or retirement. Even something as simple as passing a card around for everyone to sign is an example of a formalized process of gift-giving in the workplace.

Because the office is a professional environment, it's important to be mindful and stick to your individual workplace's rules for what is appropriate. If you have a personal relationship with a coworker outside of work and want to give them a little something extra for their birthday, or celebrate their milestone in a more extravagant way, you can always find a way to give a gift to them at a different time, preferably away from the office (or discreetly in the breakroom, while everyone is doing something else).

People tend to have strong feelings about whether or not employees should give gifts to their boss. Some argue that you're already giving your boss a gift every day with your work and that lower-paid employees should never be expected to shell out money for their (likely) much more highly compensated superior. On the other hand, some people see a group gift from the team to the boss as a way to show appreciation for their leadership and let them know you enjoy being part of the workforce they've created. Both of these arguments are valid, and the truth is you may find your office is full of people with both opinions or an opinion that's somewhere in between. Ultimately, it's up to you, your coworkers, and your established office culture as to whether or not it's appropriate to show your boss appreciation in the form of a gift. If you're organizing a group gift, be mindful that spending money on gifts for bosses or coworkers should never be mandatory, and cajoling someone into coughing up their hard-earned money to contribute is far more likely to create negative feelings than positive ones.

If you are the boss (congrats!) and you want to occasionally give gifts of appreciation to your employees, make sure you create clear guidelines about when and how that is done to ensure the gift-giving is equally accessible to all employees. Creating a policy where the top salesperson of every quarter gets an extra day of paid time off is a great, understandable, and equitable way to give back to your employees. Bringing only one of your employees a souvenir from your vacation because it reminded you of them may seem nice, but in reality, it could be taken as a show of favoritism, leading to potential discomfort for the employee that received the gift, and jealousy from those that didn't.

However, we all know gifts aren't always formalized, so we can give the people we work with less formal gifts in a variety of ways. For example:

- **Offering to grab your desk mate a coffee while you're out grabbing one for yourself.**
- **Letting someone borrow your stapler when theirs is empty.**
- **Recommending a book or article that aligns with a coworker's interests.**
- **Offering your extra phone charger to a coworker who has left theirs at home.**

Ultimately, you'll never go wrong giving your coworkers a little gift as long as you do it in a way that is respectful of everyone around you and remember to keep an eye out for social cues that might signal they don't appreciate the extra attention or that receiving gifts makes them uncomfortable.

But what about the intangible gifts we give our coworkers every day by offering help, expertise, or even just a place to vent? That's where our next love language comes in.

COWORKERS & ACTS OF SERVICE

Chances are when you're at work you already have enough on your plate focusing on, you know, your work, but keeping an eye out for ways to make our coworkers' lives easier is another way we can show a little more love in the workplace. We all know you have to put on your own oxygen mask before you can put on anyone else's, but once yours is secure and the air is flowing, there's no reason not to turn to the person next to you and make sure they're able to breathe as well.

Acts of service in the workplace don't have to be ostentatious or even take a huge amount of time. They can be something as simple as helping an older coworker with a new piece of technology you've noticed they're struggling with, or swinging by a new hire's desk to make sure they're settling in okay. Sometimes, a coworker's need for help will be more obvious, and you can really make a difference in their life by offering to switch shifts or cover their desk in an emergency. Just as we said with words of affirmation, these acts of service should come from a genuine

place, and not because you're expecting them to be able to do the same for you the moment you ask. (Though, of course, we all hope they would.)

Other acts of service you can do in the workplace include:

- **Offering to proofread a coworker's email.**
- **Taking on an extra project to give an already swamped coworker a break.**
- **Helping the new guy figure out how to use the printer.**
- **Helping the office manager take out the trash.**

Acts of service between coworkers, particularly those at the same level in the office hierarchy, can help to create an environment where everyone feels like they have each other's back. As much as TV shows and movies might glamorize the cut-throat, kill-or-be-killed office, anyone who has actually worked in one of these environments can tell you definitively that it is not a fun place to be. Work will always come with some level of stress or anxiety, but nobody wants to work in a place where they feel like they're drowning all the time. That's where acts of service come in. Acts of service between coworkers reduce competition and increase trust, leading to a better experience for everyone overall and a greater sense of teamwork. The benefits you get from doing acts of service in the workplace are the same as acts of service you do for anyone else—the satisfaction that comes from helping others, and the knowledge that you made the world a slightly better place.

With all of that in mind, it's important to remember that acts of service in the workplace should be equitable. A common refrain I often see from child-free workers is that they're regularly expected to trade their holidays to accommodate coworkers with kids, or have work dumped on them in other ways because they're assumed to have more free time than everybody else. That type of behavior is unfair at best, and discriminatory at worst. Everyone deserves time to rest and recharge, whether they're spending that free time with their children, their cat, or their favorite Netflix show.

COWORKERS & PHYSICAL TOUCH

Let's be honest. The only genuinely understood and acceptable form of physical touch in the workplace is a handshake—and after the COVID-19 pandemic even that is dicey. We're not going to say physical touch has no place in your professional life, but that place is highly limited and should exist under strict parameters. The office is a shared space, and keeping that shared space comfortable for everyone is of the utmost importance. While you may be someone who uses physical touch as your love language in most of your other relationships, the way you use it in the office will likely

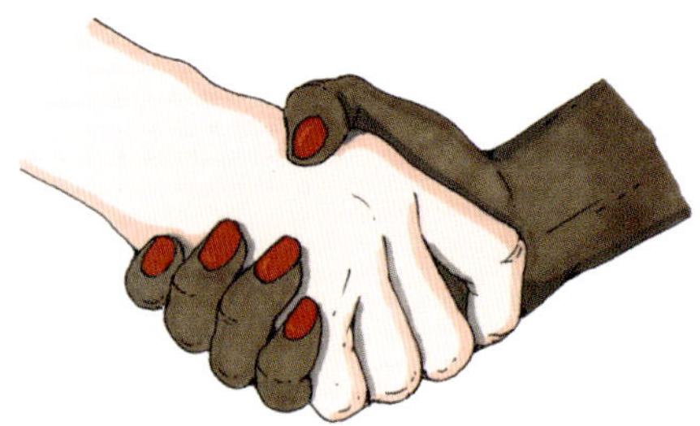

- A high five after a job well done.
- Giving a coworker a hug after a hard day (but only after asking if that's something they'd like).
- An arm around the shoulder during a team photo (again, only after checking that it's okay).

have to be adjusted for a professional environment. In short: you may be a hugger, but that doesn't mean your coworker is.

We all know the horror stories. The #MeToo movement of 2017 was full of them. Bosses who used physical touch to intimidate and abuse female employees. Coworkers who used after-hours drinks as an opportunity to push physical boundaries they never would during the workday. Generally speaking, bosses shouldn't be touching their employees, and coworkers shouldn't be touching each other.

That said, there may be appropriate places for coworkers to offer small amounts of physical touch to each other. The key word here is offer. We've already talked about how consent is key when it comes to physical touch, regardless of how close a relationship is, but it's particularly important when you're in a professional setting with people whose touch preferences would likely not be made clear to you.

Some examples of appropriate physical touch in a work environment might be:

In general, physical touch in the workplace should be limited, brief, and consent-led by both parties. In fact, respecting a coworker's physical space may actually express your love for them better than an awkward hug ever could. Which brings us to . . .

COWORKERS & RESPECTING BOUNDARIES

Boundaries are an incredibly important part of a functional workplace. Boundaries around time, appropriate conversation, email etiquette, and workload all work together to make your working environment better for everyone. Of course, we all know boundaryless work environments exist, and the stress they can cause for those who work in them.

I'm writing this from the USA, a place that famously has issues with workplace boundaries. It is not uncommon here for workers to pride themselves on staying late, working weekends, and never saying no to the boss. This always-on work environment is sometimes referred to as "hustle culture," but I think I have a better name for it: burnout culture.

As a millennial (born 1981–1996), I was often taught that things such as answering after-hours emails, unpaid internships, arriving early, and staying late were all part of what was needed to get ahead in the cut-throat corporate world. Luckily, Gen Z (born 1997–2012) is pushing back against this trend in headline-making ways. Today's young workers see what burnout culture gets us (high stress, low reward) and are choosing to prioritize their work-life balance and mental health instead. They have no problem saying no to unreasonable demands, which can sometimes lead to a culture clash between them and their older bosses, or coworkers.

When you come from a generation that was taught never to say no at work, it may seem shocking to hear an entry-level employee assert their right to leave at an appointed time or take the paid time off outlined in their contract. Sometimes, seeing someone assert a boundary that you've let get trampled in your own life can bring up feelings of shame and regret. If a twenty-year-old new hire is able to confidently say they won't answer emails after 6 p.m., why can't I? And how much time have I wasted on after-hours work assuming there was no other way? Paradigm shifts can be tough, but in the case of workplace boundaries, Gen Z has it right. A job is a job, and there will always be expectations we have to meet during working hours. But your boss does not have carte blanche to ask anything of you at any time, and workers who value their free time are not inherently less dedicated than those who refuse to take time off or who make being "busy" a core part of their identity.

> WORKERS WHO VALUE THEIR FREE TIME ARE NOT INHERENTLY LESS DEDICATED THAN THOSE WHO REFUSE TO TAKE TIME OFF.

Examples of healthy boundaries everyone has a right to set in the workplace include:

- "I only answer work emails during working hours."
- "I don't give out my personal cell-phone number."
- "I don't discuss my dating life at work."
- "I won't stay late without being paid overtime."
- "I am entitled to take the holidays outlined in my contract."
- "My workload can't accommodate any more tasks right now."

The workplace is a space where many different personalities need to find a way to coexist. People who may not naturally choose to spend time together may find themselves having to spend long hours in the same room or working closely together on a project. This only works if everyone agrees to respect each other's stated boundaries, live, and let live.

One way to help ensure your boundaries are respected at work is to make sure you're respecting the boundaries of others. We all work best when we're comfortable and able to focus on the task at hand. What creates comfort for you may look dramatically different to what creates comfort for someone else. You may not understand why your coworker prefers to eat lunch alone at their desk rather than joining you and the rest of the team out at your favorite local spot, but you don't have to. They may enjoy the quiet time as a way to recharge, they may use that hour to call a loved one or just to veg out and play a game on their phone. The reason doesn't matter–once the boundary is set, it's your job to respect it. Just as it would be their job to respect yours.

COWORKERS & EMOTIONAL SECURITY

Anyone who has dealt with an emotionally insecure person in the workplace knows how damaging they can be to the whole office environment. Conversely, anyone who has dealt with a supportive, level-headed coworker knows how much of a benefit they can be to morale. Obviously, we want to strive to be the latter. Even worse is the emotionally insecure, volatile boss, whose temper tantrums become the stuff of office legend. They may feel as though their approach is just "tough love," but it's actually abusive, and rather than motivating their team to work harder, it's doing the opposite.

Emotional insecurity can manifest in the workplace in a number of ways, such as:

- Abusive language.
- Yelling/blowups.
- Crying/freak-outs.
- Aggressive or hyperbolic emails (see also: emails sent at inappropriate hours with demands that they be responded to right away).

> BEING SOMEONE WHO YOUR COWORKERS KNOW THEY CAN GO TO FOR LEVEL-HEADED ADVICE OR FEEDBACK WILL BE RECOGNIZED AND APPRECIATED.

People work better when they're relaxed and secure. When everyone feels as if they have to walk on tiptoes at all times, it does not create a productive environment. Lack of morale affects a company's emotional health, and when a company has poor emotional health, everyone's work and productivity suffers.

Increased emotional security is actually one of the ways in which remote and hybrid work has helped people. Less time in the office means fewer opportunities for tensions to rise to an explosive level, or for personalities to clash in a way that affects and disturbs everyone. When things do get heated, everyone has the opportunity to go home and cool down, or to simply set their status to "away" and take a walk around the block. You don't always have a say in who your coworkers are (unless you're a hiring manager, in which case emotional security is a key trait you should look for), but getting space from an emotionally insecure person outside of nights and weekends can help to make dealing with them more manageable.

There will always be times of heightened workloads or anxiety in a workplace, but navigating these in a calm and centered way is better in the long run. That's why being a source of emotional security in the workplace is an act of love. Even if you have a highly volatile boss or team member, being someone who your coworkers know they can go to for level-headed advice or helpful feedback will be recognized and appreciated—even if they're not words of affirmation people, so it goes unsaid.

But what do you do when genuine differences of opinion arise that just cannot be ignored? Emotional security is great, but you'll also need our next love language to make sure disputes at work are handled in a manner that leaves everyone feeling heard, even if they don't come in.

Readers, it's time to talk about . . .

COWORKERS & HEALTHY DEBATE

Being able to hash out differences of opinion in a respectful way while at work is a crucial skill. People tend to take pride in their work, meaning they will likely have strong opinions about how things should be done, or what to prioritize to move things forward. Different personalities and values mean that coworkers may disagree fiercely on key aspects of the job, and these disagreements can sometimes get heated. That's normal. What isn't normal is resorting to insults, raised voices, or sabotage to try and get your own way.

Chances are you won't agree with your coworkers on a lot of things. From politics to parenting to who your favorite Real Housewife is, most arguments at work can be avoided by simply agreeing to disagree and getting on with your day. However, when that disagreement involves something that actually affects your work, it means you're going to have to find a way to resolve it that is productive and respectful on both sides.

> SPEAK TO YOUR COWORKERS THE WAY YOU'D WANT THEM TO SPEAK TO YOU.

Remember that healthy debate requires a genuine openness to what the other person is saying, and a willingness to be wrong or (as the kids would say) "take the L" if you get outvoted or proven wrong. It may be a hard pill to swallow, but sometimes your coworker may have expertise on a particular matter that actually makes their opinion more valuable than yours. Sometimes, the person with the greater level of expertise is you, and you'll need to find a way to calmly explain your position without being condescending. In general, the golden rule always applies: speak to your coworkers the way you'd want them to speak to you.

If you and your coworker find yourselves on opposite sides of an argument, try using phrases such as:

- "I hear what you're saying."
- "I respect your opinion on this."
- "Let me think about what you just said."

In the case of a particularly intractable argument, it may be time to ask for a third party to weigh in. Luckily, this is what your manager, boss, or other team members are for. When bringing in others to provide an opinion on a disagreement, it's important to keep emotional security at the forefront. Nobody wants to feel as if they're being dragged into the middle of a heated fight, or that they're being used to take

potshots at somebody who they also have to maintain a functional working relationship with. You can feel strongly that your idea is best or your course of action makes the most sense, and you can argue strongly in your own favor, while still maintaining respect for your coworker and their take on things.

And if the person on the other end of the argument can't do the same? Well, that's what HR is for. At the end of the day, the only person whose behavior you can control is your own, and any good boss will know how to handle someone who is behaving inappropriately over what should be a professional disagreement. In a functional workplace, even people who disagree should at least be on the same page about wanting the best for your company's goals.

And now that we've said the "G" word, it's time to talk about . . .

COWORKERS & SHARED GOALS & EXPERIENCES

Ultimately, your company's mission is a goal that everyone in the workplace should share. This can be anything from being the best in your field to making the best latte in your area, to the more universal goal of simply wanting to stay in business and stay employed. Whatever it is you do, there is likely something that you and your coworkers are all explicitly working toward.

You probably already know what your shared goals with your coworkers are, as your company likely makes them clear repeatedly. There are metrics you need to hit, profits you need to make, accounts you need to land–and working together to meet these goals can lead to a feeling of accomplishment for everyone. So, how do we ensure that shared goals help us bond and show love to our coworkers? By celebrating when they're met, of course!

When I was a kid, every year my elementary school would hold a competition to see which class could read the most pages during reading time. The class that had read the most pages at the end of the year for every grade was given its own pizza party. What kid doesn't want a pizza party? As a voracious reader myself, I never felt more appreciated in the classroom than when I would go to the front to log my new reading pages, being cheered on by the rest of my classmates. I swelled with pride knowing that, when the time came for my class to collect its gooey, cheesy reward, I was a big part of making that happen.

So, why not try something similar in your office? Sure, a pizza party may not be the motivator that it once was (or maybe it is–who doesn't love pizza?), but finding fun ways to celebrate collective wins can help everyone in the office bond over a shared sense of accomplishment, and engage in some hard-earned on-the-clock down time. (As an added bonus, this also counts as quality time with your coworkers–it's two love languages for the price of one!) Once a shared goal is accomplished, it's important not to just acknowledge the team, but also the individuals who went the extra mile to make it happen. Even something as simple as shouting out a coworker by name in the office Slack channel can help them feel as if they've contributed to the collective in a meaningful, recognized way.

Wait, that sounds a lot like words of affirmation! Now we're getting three love languages for the price of one! It's a love-language bonanza!

Shared experiences also come naturally to coworkers. It's one of the benefits of spending so many hours together in the same place! Oftentimes, it's the toughest shared work experiences that bond coworkers together the most.

Some common shared experiences between coworkers include:

- Venting about an overly long meeting that could have been an email.
- Laughing during after-work drinks about a quirky client.
- Sharing your theories on the mystery of who keeps stealing all the string cheese from the fridge.
- Reminiscing about last summer's Great Fire Drill Fiasco.

Ultimately, these are all ways that coworkers can use the love language of shared experiences to get closer to one another. Even if we have much more intimate relationships with family and friends, it can sometimes be hard to fully explain our work to them, or the unique personalities we encounter while trying to do it. On this score, sometimes your coworkers are the only people who truly understand what you mean when you discuss a complicated work issue and are the only people who truly understand all the additional factors needed to give good advice.

SOMETIMES YOUR COWORKERS ARE THE ONLY PEOPLE WHO TRULY UNDERSTAND WHAT YOU MEAN WHEN YOU DISCUSS A COMPLICATED WORK ISSUE.

In this way, shared experiences can lead to a shared language all of you can use to express love at work.

One last note before we move on to your next quiz: be careful that shared experiences don't lead to toxic gossip. Venting is fun, but if it becomes something that affects how you're interacting during the workday it's time to pull it back. Workplaces can sometimes rival the schoolyard as hotbeds of toxic bullying, especially when coworkers are using their shared annoyance at one particular person as a way to bond. Smack talk is the opposite of a love language, and although we all engage in it from time to time, it has the potential to do a lot more harm than good if it's happening often or only directed at one person. Ultimately, your workplace should be a professional environment.

QUIZ

WORK LOVE LANGUAGES

Still not sure exactly how you like to show love in the office? Luckily, we've got a quiz ready to help you figure it out. Maybe you could even snap a pic of the quiz and drop a link in your office chat for coworkers to find out their preferred office love languages for themselves!

Read each of the following statements and circle the answer that best describes you, then turn to page 156 to discover your Work Love Languages preferences.

C My biggest work pet peeve is after-hours emails.

A My biggest work pet peeve is someone who always has to be right.

H My biggest work pet peeve is a coworker who only looks out for themself.

F My biggest work pet peeve is when someone doesn't say "thank you."

A I love a job that really challenges me.

G I love a job that rewards me in tangible ways.

E I love a job where I get to be in the office with coworkers.

I I love a job where my coworkers are friends off the clock.

I The worst type of coworker is one who is all business all the time.

D The worst type of coworker is one who can't handle stress.

E The worst type of coworker is one who calls out sick all the time.

B The worst type of coworker is one who won't work as a team.

C I like when my workplace has clear rules and protocols.

B I like when my workplace has clear goals and metrics.

G I like when my employer rewards hard work.

H I like when my workplace is non-competitive and team-oriented.

F My best days at work are the ones where I get a shout-out from the boss.

B My best days at work are the ones where I meet a goal.

A My best days at work are the ones where my idea is chosen.

I My best day at work is the office holiday party.

H I love feeling helpful at work.

G I love being rewarded at work.

E I love feeling comfortable at work.

D I love feeling secure at work.

C I can't work somewhere that doesn't respect my time.

D I can't work somewhere that is always stressful.

A I can't work somewhere that won't listen to new ideas.

I I can't work somewhere without friends.

F I love a compliment box.

E I love a high five.

G I love a secret Santa.

I I love a team dinner.

B Nothing bonds me to a coworker like an inside joke.

D Nothing bonds me to a coworker like seeing them calm in a crisis.

A Nothing bonds me to a coworker like good-natured competition.

H Nothing bonds me to a coworker like knowing I can ask them for help.

D I care most about my workplace's culture.

B I care most about my workplace's achievements and reputation.

F I care most about being recognized for my accomplishments.

G I care most about my workplace's benefits.

At a job interview, I'm asking about . . .

C Company policies.

B Expectations and future plans.

H Workplace culture.

E Hybrid/remote options.

F Processes for feedback and mentorship.

LOVE LANGUAGES IN EVERYDAY LIFE

Alright, folks, we've come to what may be the most important section of the entire book. (Funny how we authors tend to put that at the end, eh?) We've talked about how to show love to our romantic partners, friends, family, and coworkers, but now it's time to ask what may be the most vital question of all: how do we show love to all the other humans we encounter in our everyday lives?

We've talked a lot about the loneliness epidemic already. All around us, the world seems to have become a more uncertain, unfriendly place. So, how can we remedy this? At the risk of sounding clichéd, what if all we need is love? The way we carry ourselves in public and the way we treat the random people we meet on the street, the clerk at the grocery store, or even the person stuck next to us in traffic can have a much bigger impact than we might think. The onus is on all of us to make the world a more friendly, loving place. Once the menu of love is open to everyone, we may see more opportunities to order from it in our day-to-day lives.

Who doesn't want to live in a more loving, kind world? Creating that starts with us. We can't force other people to order off the menu of love or to become fluent in all the love languages, but we can control how much love we inject into the world by using the love languages ourselves.

That, dear readers, is the real power of love in our everyday lives, and it cannot be understated.

> ONCE THE MENU OF LOVE IS OPEN TO EVERYONE, WE MAY SEE MORE OPPORTUNITIES TO ORDER FROM IT IN OUR DAY-TO-DAY LIVES.

EVERYDAY WORDS OF AFFIRMATION

Words of affirmation are one of the easiest love languages for us to use with people we barely know or are not intimate with. It costs nothing to be generous with your compliments or to let people know how they have brightened your day (thereby brightening their day in return). Public life provides us with infinite opportunities to share a kind word with a fellow human. All you have to do is choose to notice. Notice if the clerk who is bagging your groceries went the extra mile to make sure everything is securely packed, notice when your favorite barista changes up their latte art, notice when your server at the diner did a great job and tell the manager on your way out.

Obviously, this doesn't just apply to the various workers we encounter as we're going about our daily life. We can also be generous with compliments to anyone we meet. Anyone who's had their outfit complimented by a stranger on the street can tell you of the power that compliment can hold. So, how can we thread more words of affirmation into our everyday lives? Easy!

- Tell the guy you see on the street with cool sneakers that you like his shoes.
- Let the person you see reading on the train know that you also read that book and loved it!
- *Definitely* tell the mom on your flight who's struggling to keep a fussy baby quiet how great a job she's doing.

Worried about making things awkward? I totally get it. When it comes to these types of interactions, brevity is your friend. Keep it short and sweet—be ready to deliver your compliments and be on your way. Lingering or trying to impose a conversation on someone that you don't know, may turn what could be a nice interaction into something confusing or stressful.

For all its flaws, social media also provides us with opportunities to send a nice word to a stranger. Sure, when you think about "strangers on social media" your mind probably doesn't immediately jump to examples of kind, loving behavior, but that doesn't have to be the case. As someone who built a career making comedy videos for social media, I know how dicey a comment section full of strangers' inner thoughts can get. That said, I also know how much it can mean getting a kind comment from someone who enjoyed my post. Let the people you follow know that their video made you laugh or think. Leave a comment telling the blogger whose recipe you loved, how much you enjoyed it. So much of the internet is taken up with people using anonymity as a shield to be mean, but it doesn't have to be—you can create a positive space online. Posting something nice only takes a few seconds, and you're making someone else's day better and the internet a better place in the process.

In short, an offhand compliment you give a stranger may be the thing that turns their day around.

EVERYDAY QUALITY TIME

Make the moments you spend in someone else's life matter, even if it's just half an hour on the train or an exchange of smiles as you pass each other on the street. Quality time with strangers isn't about locking eyes and agreeing to go off on a grand adventure (although you could do that, too), rather it's about being open to interactions with new people and committing yourself to being a positive force when those opportunities arise.

SO MUCH OF THE INTERNET IS TAKEN UP WITH PEOPLE USING ANONYMITY AS A SHIELD TO BE MEAN, BUT IT DOESN'T HAVE TO BE.

It's about the art of chitchat—from casual conversations in line at the pharmacy to a few words exchanged on your daily commute. Some people are disparaging about "small talk," but do you know what another word for small talk is? Pleasantries. Why? Because these small conversations aren't about going deep or establishing intimacy; they're about creating small, pleasant moments between people sharing the same space. For example:

- Chatting about the weather while you wait for the bus.
- Asking a fellow dog owner if your pups can say "Hi."
- Stopping to chat with an acquaintance, if you see them on the street.

Don't be a stranger to strangers. Leave yourself open to sharing small moments of connection with humanity—introduce yourself, or say hello to your neighbor as they pass you on the street. If you want to go deeper, try showing up for community events, from block parties to board meetings, and taking some time to meet the people around you. It can seem as if the concept of neighborliness is all but dead, but we can revive it through our actions and by dedicating just a little bit of our own time to improving the quality of life around us.

EVERYDAY GIFTS

Chances are you don't spend your days walking up to random strangers offering them gifts (unless you're a TikToker and that's your schtick, in which case, rock on!), but that doesn't mean that gifts can't play a role in how we interact with our neighbors, acquaintances, and even full-blown strangers. In order to see all the opportunities we have to give gifts to those around us, we may need to explore our definition of a "gift." A gift doesn't have to come with a card or be wrapped in a bow. When it comes to giving back to our community, a gift includes things such as:

- **Leaving a little something in the tip jar at your favorite cafe.**
- **Donating clothes, foods, or other goods to your local shelter.**
- **Donating your time to clean up a local park.**
- **Contributing financially to charities, community projects, and scholarships.**
- **Lending your artistic talent to paint a mural or other beautification projects.**
- **Lending your knowledge or expertise to help advance a community cause.**

There are so many ways we can give back to our communities, and most of them will only cost us our time. One example of inter-community gift exchanges that I see all over my neighborhood in Brooklyn are little free libraries. These "libraries" consist of weather-proofed wooden boxes, usually hand-built by a community member, installed in a public space such as a park or garden, where neighbors are encouraged to take and leave free books for each other. Every quarter, I take stock of my own home library to decide on a few titles I can part with and bring them over to the little free library at the end of my block. Sometimes, the books stay there for months at a time. Sometimes they're scooped up right away, and I get to enjoy the feeling of knowing one of my neighbors is reading a new book because of me.

EVERYDAY ACTS OF SERVICE

Acts of service are one of the best ways to build a better, more loving world—and are another great way to give back to and strengthen the community around you. In fact, without acts of service, we wouldn't have community at all. Community is built brick by brick, with millions of tiny little acts of service every single day. Acts of service that build community can be as simple as:

- **Holding the door open for a stranger.**
- **Spotting an elderly neighbor who lives alone, and offering to help them mow the lawn or bring their groceries inside.**
- **Watering your neighbors' plants while they're out of town, or checking in on their cat when they're not around.**
- **Opening the door and listening patiently to a canvasser as they explain why they want you to sign their petition.**

Nowadays, it's easier than ever to isolate ourselves from our community. We can have our groceries delivered instead of going to the store. We can work from home instead of walking out to our car, where we may have to say hi to a neighbor or chitchat in the driveway. We can even conduct whole friendships entirely online. While there are benefits to the rise in online life, there are downsides, too. For some, the rise in online relationships has led to heightened anxiety around maintaining their relationships in real life. Yes, our screens can connect us, but they can also act as a shield to hide behind, keeping us safely tucked away indoors instead of engaging with the world outside our walls. Now, we all have to be much more intentional about making sure that we spend time in our community, and ensuring that time is well spent and enriching for everyone. That's where acts of service come in.

At the start of 2025, in the wake of a series of devastating wildfires, the people of Los Angeles witnessed just how important acts of service within a community can be. These ranged from volunteering to hand out water bottles or collect donations, to literally saving strangers from burning buildings. These acts of service were often highly localized,

BE CONSCIENTIOUS IN THE WAY YOU MOVE AROUND THE WORLD.

with neighbors helping neighbors process the devastation and grief, but they were also global. I'll never forget seeing a line around the block in my own neighborhood in Brooklyn to donate clothes and other essentials to fire victims on the other side of the country. While the loss and sadness caused by the fires will stay with the victims forever, so, too, will the hope created by seeing a community come together to help each other.

New York City can sometimes get a reputation for being cold or unfeeling, but the truth is, without a sense of community the city would fall apart. There are so many of us so close together we have to care about each other—even if it's just to ensure that we all get on the train in the most efficient way possible. It's not uncommon to see a stranger walk up to the entrance to the subway and wordlessly help a mother bring her stroller up the stairs and continue on with their commute. People give up their seats for pregnant women and the elderly every day. I've had buses and train doors held for me more times than I can count. Even in one of the busiest cities in the world, it's little acts of service that keep the sense of community strong.

EVERYDAY PHYSICAL TOUCH

I'll get this out of the way right up top: I'm not about to tell you to go around touching strangers. I think we can all agree nobody wants that. Instead, we can reframe this love language to mean the way we share space with one another every day. It's about being mindful of the environment that we're in and doing our best to make it as comfortable as possible for everyone.

We've all been at a party with someone who lacks spatial awareness—they're bumping into you, they're stepping on toes, or they're talking at a volume that means no one else gets to have anything to say. It sucks! Nobody enjoys being around that person. So, don't be that person. Instead, be conscientious in the way you move around the world and, as the Girl Scouts would say, leave every place a little better than you found it.

Think about things such as:

- **Moving your bag out of the way so someone else can sit down.**
- **Not bringing a tuna molt on the plane.**
- **Not blocking the aisle at the grocery store.**
- **Always cleaning up after yourself and picking up your trash. (Side note: can you believe there are still people who litter?)**

These are all small ways that we can be physically aware of one another to show respect and, yes, love to the people around us. In writing this section, I've thought a lot about what it means to be a physical being in public. There's a common sentiment among young people online about "not wanting to be perceived." While it's said as a joke, it highlights a core emotion that we all feel sometimes: being out in public is hard. So, why not try to make "public" a better place for everyone by being courteous, careful, and physically aware?

RESPECTING BOUNDARIES EVERYDAY

Respecting boundaries is another important way in which we can create a safe, comfortable community for ourselves and others. Without wanting to sound like your college philosophy professor, what is a society, if not a group of people agreeing to live within a particular set of boundaries? Generally, laws are the boundaries that we've all put in place for behavior that keeps us safe. That's not to say that every law is just or good, but that's a larger conversation for a different book. However, the big laws—the ones we all agree on, such as don't murder, steal, or kick somebody's dog—represent long-standing rules that human beings have laid down to keep themselves and others safe.

Yet, it's not only by following laws that we can show that we respect our communities. You can also show appreciation for your community by observing other boundaries, such as:

- Keeping quiet hours in your apartment complex.
- Staying on top of trash collection day.
- Keeping the front of your home pleasant to look at.

Travel is an excellent time to practice many languages, including the love languages. You've probably heard the proverb "When in Rome, do as the Romans do," as an expression of the importance of blending into the norms and culture of a country you are visiting. It not only makes your travels smoother, but it also shows respect for the place that you are choosing to visit. Tourists who get a bad reputation are generally the ones who refuse to do this, instead trying to impose their home country's norms on everyone else.

I come from a place that is distinctly not well-regarded for its tourist behavior. (Sorry to my fellow American tourists, but you know it's true. And sorry again to the woman who shushed me at a bar in Berlin for being American-level loud in a German-quiet space. That was my bad . . .) For this reason, I try to be especially mindful of the norms in a place, when traveling. I look up the local culture, learn a few crucial words and phrases, such as "Hello," "Thank you," "Where's the bathroom?," and "Sorry, I don't speak the language because I am a dumb American." On a recent trip to Poland (with a friend to go see Taylor Swift's Eras Tour–shared experiences, baby!), my pre-trip research turned up multiple Reddit posts about getting fined for jaywalking in Warsaw. As a New Yorker, skilled in crossing the street whenever I damn well please, I had to make a mental note not to exercise my jaywalking powers while on vacation, even if I saw a perfectly good opportunity to cross. While traveling I do my best to change myself for the place that I'm in, rather than expecting the place to change for me.

Except for that one time at the bar in Germany–*Es tut mir leid.*

> WHAT IS A SOCIETY, IF NOT A GROUP OF PEOPLE AGREEING TO LIVE WITHIN A PARTICULAR SET OF BOUNDARIES?

EVERYDAY EMOTIONAL SECURITY

Behave in a way that makes the people around you feel safe. It's really that simple. We've all been in situations where someone was behaving in an erratic way in public, and I think we can all agree that it is stressful at best, and genuinely terrifying at worst. We've all seen viral videos of people having over-the-top meltdowns because the Apple store couldn't fix their phone or they're being escorted off a plane. (Or maybe that's just my TikTok algorithm.) Road rage is another great example of how emotional volatility in a public space can create an unsafe situation for everyone—even if the person ahead did totally cut you off.

However, it's not just explosive situations, such as two guys fighting at the bar or the couple yelling at each other in public, that contribute to a lack of emotional security. Sometimes, we may find ourselves in a situation that just, objectively, sucks. Perhaps we're stuck on the tarmac at the end of a long flight, or maybe the card reader at the grocery store went down at the exact wrong time. Perhaps we're just having a bad day and every little thing feels like a personal attack. I get it. I've been there—and I'm the last person in the world to tell you that you should be all smiles all the time (I'm pretty sure my friends would laugh me out of town, if I tried). That said, maintaining a baseline of emotional security as we move through the world means that we won't make a bad situation worse. Getting into an argument with a customer service rep about a misdelivered sock order, isn't going to make your day any better, and being the person who aggressively honks their way through traffic won't actually make it move any faster.

Being kind and level-headed, even in frustrating situations, can make a huge difference for everyone around you, but they're not the only people who benefit. You provide emotional security for yourself when you try to stay grounded in annoying situations and remain calm, even in a tense or chaotic environment.

Not sure how to do this? Try some of these science-backed, totally invisible ways to center yourself in public:

- **Box breathing.** A relaxation technique, where you breathe in cycles of four seconds. Inhale for four, hold for four, exhale for four, hold for four, and repeat.
- **5-4-3-2-1 grounding.** A mindfulness exercise in which you mentally list five things you see, four things you feel, three things you hear, two things you smell, and one thing you taste in order to ground yourself in the present moment.
- **Body scan.** Take a moment to mentally scan your body from head to toe, noticing any sensations along the way. You can also subtly tense and release each muscle as you scan it, if you're in a place where that feels comfortable.
- **Keep a gratitude journal.** Okay, so maybe journaling in the moment isn't always feasible. Nonetheless, keeping a gratitude journal has long-term effects that will help you focus on the positive even during tough or frustrating situations.

But what to do when conflict is unavoidable? Luckily, we have our next love language to guide us.

EVERYDAY HEALTHY DEBATE

There are many ways to have healthy, intellectually stimulating debates with a neighbor. Perhaps the two of you root for different sports teams and engage each other in some lighthearted ribbing before the big game. Maybe you've found yourselves on opposite sides of a local issue and talking it out can help both of you clarify how you feel. Maybe you're both just two people who like to argue and have found kindred spirits in each other. The point is, there are plenty of healthy,

> BEING KIND AND LEVEL-HEADED, EVEN IN FRUSTRATING SITUATIONS, CAN MAKE A HUGE DIFFERENCE FOR EVERYONE AROUND YOU.

non-confrontational ways we may find ourselves engaging in debates with our neighbours every day.

Unfortunate, it is also true that you will occasionally come into conflict with people around you—from neighbors to other drivers to the drunk girl who just accidentally cut you in line at the bar. As a non-confrontational person by nature, I try to avoid these types of situations as much as possible but conflict is simply a fact of life and we all should try to work on how we behave when it arises. It can be easy to become the worst version of ourselves because we don't have the same level of care for the person on the other end of the conflict as we do for friends, family, or romantic partners. So, how do we treat everyone (even a stranger who is really testing our patience) with respect in conflict?

It's time to start speaking the love language of healthy debate.

> AS WE MOVE THROUGH THE WORLD, WE SHOULD ASSUME EVERYONE HAS THE SAME GOAL TO LIVE A HAPPY AND FULFILLING LIFE.

Picture this: you're walking through a crowded coffee shop when suddenly someone walks right smack dab into you. Their coffee spills everywhere, including on your white shirt. The other person suddenly starts yelling about how you need to watch where you're going. Suddenly, the whole coffee shop is watching and waiting to see how you'll react.

Maintaining your composure in a high-tension situation like this may seem like a tall order. It may even seem unfair! They bumped into you, after all! That's why it's important to see these moments of interpersonal conflict as an opportunity to show your character. Can you treat someone with respect, even if they're not doing the same to you? Can you stand your ground calmly without letting yourself get upset? Obviously, you have the right to remove yourself from a disrespectful conversation or a situation where you feel unsafe, but there is power in not letting an aggressive person drag you down to their level.

At the very least, the people around you will be impressed.

EVERYDAY SHARED GOALS & EXPERIENCES

How can I share goals with a stranger, you ask. It may seem odd to think about, but the truth is you actually share goals with strangers all the time. Do you want to live in a functional society? Chances are that's a goal you share with most people around you. Want the bus to arrive on time? So does the lady next to you.

As we move through the world, we should assume everyone has the same goal to live a happy and fulfilling life. Though the definition of a happy and fulfilling life may look different from person to person, it's humanizing to remember that we're all just out there doing our best for ourselves and our loved ones.

So, how can we work to speak the love language of shared goals within our community? Try some of the following:

- **Join a local organization with a clear mission, such as opening a new park or building more affordable housing.**
- **Join a beautification group that picks up trash on weekends.**
- **Help a neighbor shovel the sidewalk, so that it's clear for everyone to use.**

Shared experiences are another major way we connect to new people every single day. On a fundamental level, if someone is in the same space as you, they're sharing an experience with you. It's important to keep yourself open to shared experiences with strangers. Sometimes the most beautiful moments can be when you and a stranger momentarily bond over something strange or interesting that you just saw together. Perhaps you are sitting on the same park bench when a particularly beautiful bird flies by, or you share a laugh because that same bird swoops down and steals somebody's sandwich. Maybe you're just indulging in the simple joy of complaining about prices with somebody in line at the grocery store.

When it comes to using the love languages in everyday life, it's these little moments of human connection that really count. These moments may be fleeting, and they may look much different to how we express love in our more intimate relationships, but each one represents a powerful opportunity to inject just a little more love into the world around us.

QUIZ EVERYDAY LOVE LANGUAGES

Still not sure how each of the love languages ranks in your everyday life? It's time for your final love language quiz, which will tell you everything you need to know about how you like to express love in public.

Read each of the following statements and then circle the answer that best describes you. Turn to page 156 to tally your answers and discover your Everyday Love Languages preferences.

F I want to live in a community that is fun.
H I want to live in a community that is safe.
A I want to live in a community where everyone has each other's backs.
E I want to live in a community that is growing.

I I try to be mindful of rules and etiquette in public.
E I try to be open to moments of connection in public.
D I try to be mindful of my space in public.
B I try to look out for ways to give back in public.

G I'm good in a crisis.
C I'm good at making other people smile.
D I'm good at making people feel comfortable.
F I'm good at meeting new people.

I The best neighbors are considerate.
G The best neighbors know how to work out differences.
B The best neighbors give back to the community.
A The best neighbors are happy to lend a helping hand.

B Community is generosity.
H Community is safety.
I Community is trust.
A Community is selflessness.

G Sometimes I think I'd make a great hostage negotiator.

F Sometimes I think I'd make a great event planner.

I Sometimes I think I'd make a great judge.

C Sometimes I think I'd make a great hype man.

E My community makes me feel proud.

H My community makes me feel safe.

G My community makes me feel heard.

I My community makes me feel respected.

Out in public you're most likely to hear me say . . .

C "Oooh, I love those shoes!"

D "Excuse me!"

F "Nice to meet you!"

A "Can I help you with that?"

D I'm always mindful of my space in public.

H I'm always mindful of my energy in public.

G I'm always mindful of my words in public.

E I'm always mindful of my contributions in public.

H Angry people stress me out.

E Anti-social people stress me out.

C Indifferent people stress me out.

B Selfish people stress me out.

A Doing things for my neighbors makes me feel fulfilled.

B Giving things to my neighbors makes me feel fulfilled.

F Getting to know my neighbors makes me feel fulfilled.

D Sharing space with my neighbors makes me feel fulfilled.

C Being kind to my neighbors makes me feel fulfilled.

QUIZ ANSWERS

And now . . . the moment you've all been waiting for . . . your quiz results! Tally up how many times each letter appears and you'll get a ranking of how much each love language resonates with you. Remember, this ranking represents your menu of love, not a set-in-stone identity marker for your entire life. Use your quiz results as an opportunity to learn, reflect, and dig deeper into how you love to love.

QUIZ ANSWERS

Tally up your answers and you'll have a good idea of how these new love languages rank for you in this moment. Come back to these answers any time you think your rankings may have changed.

NEW ROMANTIC LOVE LANGUAGES (pages 76-77)

__ A Shared Goals & Experiences

__ B Healthy Debate

__ C Emotional Security

__ D Respecting Boundaries

FRIENDSHIP LOVE LANGUAGES (pages 100-101)

__ A Respecting Boundaries

__ B Emotional Security

__ C Healthy Debate

__ D Shared Goals & Experiences

__ E Quality Time

__ F Physical Touch

__ G Words of Affirmation

__ H Receiving Gifts

__ I Acts of Service

FAMILY LOVE LANGUAGES (pages 118-119)

_ A Quality Time
_ B Physical Touch
_ C Words of Affirmation
_ D Receiving Gifts
_ E Acts of Service
_ F Respecting Boundaries
_ G Emotional Security
_ H Healthy Debate
_ I Shared Goals & Experiences

WORK LOVE LANGUAGES (pages 136-137)

_ A Healthy Debate
_ B Shared Goals & Experiences
_ C Respecting Boundaries
_ D Emotional Security
_ E Physical Touch
_ F Words of Affirmation
_ G Receiving Gifts
_ H Acts of Service
_ I Quality Time

EVERYDAY LOVE LANGUAGES (pages 152-153)

_ A Acts of Service
_ B Receiving Gifts
_ C Words of Affirmation
_ D Physical Touch
_ E Shared Goals & Experiences
_ F Quality Time
_ G Healthy Debate
_ H Emotional Security
_ I Respecting Boundaries

INDEX

For Abrams:
Editor: Sarah Robbins
Design Manager: Danielle Youngsmith
Managing Editor: Krista Keplinger
Production Manager: Larry Pekarek

Conceived, edited, and designed by Quarto Publishing, an imprint of The Quarto Group.

For Quarto:
Commissioning Editor: Jo Lightfoot
Assistant Editor: Elinor Ward
Copyeditor: Julia Shone
Design: Hello Daly
Designer: Eliana Holder
Illustrator: Ana Jarén
Production Manager: David Hearn
Managing Editor: Emma Harverson
Art Director: Martina Calvio
Publisher: Lorraine Dickey

Library of Congress Control Number: 2025933172

ISBN: 978-1-4197-8345-6
eISBN: 979-8-88707-823-6

Printed and bound in China
10 9 8 7 6 5 4 3 2 1

Abrams books are available at special discounts when purchased in quantity for premiums and promotions as well as fundraising or educational use. Special editions can also be created to specification. For details, contact specialsales@abramsbooks.com or the address below.

Abrams® is a registered trademark of Harry N. Abrams, Inc.

ABRAMS is represented in the UK and Europe by Abrams & Chronicle Books, 1 West Smithfield, London EC1A 9JU and Média-Participations, 57 rue Gaston Tessier, 75166 Paris, France.
www.abramsandchronicle.co.uk and
www.media-participations.com
info@abramsandchronicle.co.uk

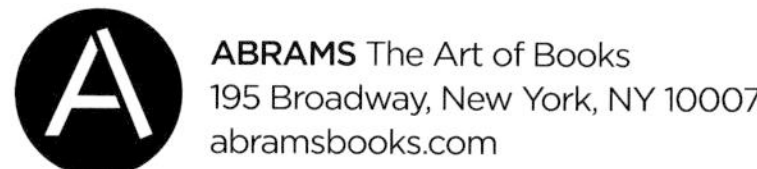